MW00623670

The Soul's Fight

Wrestling with Forgiveness

Josee D'Amore

JOSEE D'AMORE

Licensed Marriage & Family Therapist

Partnership
Publications

www.H2HP.com

–

The Soul's Fight: Wrestling with Forgiveness
by Josee D'Amore

Copyright © 2024 by Josee D'Amore
Second Edition

Partnership Publications
A Division of House to House Publications
www.H2HP.com

ISBN: 978-1-7330137-6-5

–

DEDICATION

for the salvation and healing
of many souls.

ACKNOWLEDGEMENTS

We all have those key mentors who shape us and mold us into who we are today. I am blessed to have two amazing such mentors in my life: Youth With A Mission and Pastor Wayne Corderio of New Hope Christian Fellowship. I consider them my spiritual parents since they built my foundation of faith that has never faltered. I shudder to think where my life would be today without these two influences. I am deeply thankful for both. It is a rare opportunity to publicly thank significant people in your life. I am profoundly grateful to have such a moment.

I want to thank Youth With A Mission (YWAM) for investing in my life in a profound and life altering way. What I learned from YWAM enhanced my relationship not only with God, but with others and with myself forever. One of the most revealing and inspiring lessons learned from YWAM was that God has a specific purpose for my life. And, since He has a specific purpose for my life, I could expect God to speak into my life: to guide, direct, and care for me. I also learned the benefits of prayer – how to pray and how to interact with the Living God. My world view was formed through YWAM. YWAM formed within me a heart of compassion for the people groups of the world, setting me on a journey of prayer for them that continues even today. I learned that God loves every person and people group, and that He has a divine purpose for each one that mirrors His very character. YWAM instilled a vibrant, living faith within me that has sustained me throughout my years. I often return to those lessons in my life and apply them to present circumstances.

I also want to thank New Hope Christian Fellowship and especially its founder, Pastor Wayne Cordeiro, for demonstrating the heart of God to heal His people. I had the privilege of being a part of New Hope for seven years. Those years correspond with my journey of healing and growth. It was during those years in my life that I began to feel safe, loved, and cared for. I was also encouraged to trust God for my healing. Pastor Wayne Cordeiro mirrored the heart of God towards me even when I am sure it was difficult to love me. He assured me that the benefits of opening my heart to God's touch would overpower any risk of fear or shame I might feel. He believed that God had a better plan for me than living in brokenness. He pointed me towards God's purpose for my life. He held hope for my healing when I couldn't even believe it myself. He loved me with the profound love of Jesus Christ. Thank you, Pastor Wayne Cordeiro, for your gentleness, patience, compassion, purity, care, love, and kindness towards me and for your faith in God to take all the broken pieces of my heart and make me whole again. You have impacted my life forever. I treasure you with a deeply thankful heart.

~ Introduction ~

God delights in taking hurts, wounds, and offenses and turning them into beauty as a demonstration of His power and great love for His people. The Bible as well as countless personal accounts show that God has been doing this throughout the ages. He relentlessly pursues each person, driven by a desperate love for us. I have experienced God's love pursue me in an immensely powerful way. However, I know that what God does in one life is never meant just for that one life; it is intended to impact the lives around them as well.

I share my story here not for the purpose of sensation (you won't find that here!), but to bring glory and honor to the ONE who saved me and healed me: Jesus Christ. I was utterly broken and with little hope. But then He touched me, breathed new life into me, and rebuilt me into who I am today.

I am not special. I am not different. I am not the exception. He didn't heal me because of something about me. He healed me because of who HE is. He delights in bringing wholeness to His people. He delights in restoring a person back to His original design for him or her.

Due to the fallen nature of humankind, our five senses are not able to connect us to God. God is an unseen presence; we can't touch Him, feel Him, hear Him or see Him with our natural senses. We interact with Him and sense His presence only by way of faith. That poses some challenges for all of us at times. And so it is that we often learn of Him and come to terms with Him through the stories and testimonies of what He has done in the lives of others.

I confidently and joyfully invite you to pursue God through these pages. I urge you to walk this path with sheer determination; to know Him, no matter what it takes! I challenge you to broaden your vision of who He is and what He is willing to do in your life, because He is! He has been waiting for you with desperate love. It hasn't been you waiting for Him to be willing. No. He demonstrated t willingness on the cross. It is He who waits for you! He is waiting for you even now.

It is my hope and prayer that God will take the illustrations and experiences written in these pages and use them to speak to your soul. I earnestly pray that you will have an undeniable and life-changing encounter with the Living God as you read. I pray that if you do not yet know Him as Savior, you will be embarking on a personal relationship with Jesus Christ before you finish the book.* I pray that my story will eradicate any false notions of what forgiveness is and that you will joyfully embrace this powerful and transformational gift. I pray that you will encounter Him as Redeemer, which means both Savior and Healer. He is truly both-in-one! I pray that you will open your heart and allow Him to rebuild your life in His very own way.

All the hurts, wounds, and offenses that I will share in this book have been deeply healed by the love and power of Jesus Christ. I share not from hurt but from health, not from sorrow but from joy, for God has long since brought healing into my life, rooted in the gift of forgiveness.

See Appendix A for a prayer of salvation

SECTION ONE
The Darkness

The Soul's Fight

A word, A thought, A feeling
A beam of light in the darkest corner of the heart.
The Truth!

> With the light the darkness was threatened.
> The fight began!

The fight for freedom. The fight for wholeness.
The fight to be set free!

> The chains were rattled. The bondage was pierced.
> The heart was shaken.
> Satan declared war!

The cry was louder. The prayer was stronger.
The knees were sturdy.
The Angels came!

> The soul was strengthened. The spirit was lifted.
> The heart surrendered.
> The counter-attacked released!

The cry was silenced. The prayer was choked.
The knees were wobbly.
Darkness consumed!

> The Hand reached out. The warriors fought.
> The spirit was revived.
> The Light prevailed!

Sight was restored. The bondage was lifted.
The heart rejoiced!
God's character was proven!
Great is His Faithfulness!

> The chains were broken. The war had been won.
> The soul and spirit had been set free.
> He whom the Lord sets free is free indeed!

A word. A thought. A feeling. Light!
> The Truth!

The Soul's Fight

~ Life Unraveling ~

I stood over my mom's hospital bed, exhausted and silent. It had been a grueling twenty-four hours of being at her side as she was dying. I had watched her take her last natural breath just several hours prior. A code blue had been called and nurses and doctors immediately flooded the room. As I stood just outside the doorway looking into the room, watching all the commotion of attempting to save her life, it was as if I saw her spirit leave her body. She was finally free and at peace.

I then found a vacant room nearby and slipped quietly into its welcome refuge. I sat on the floor, knees close to my body, my arms wrapped around them, sobbing my heart out. I'm rather certain I screamed some, too. It was the first time in more than twenty-four hours that I was actually alone. I don't even remember eating during that time. The rest of my family arrived soon after the code blue was called, and I explained to all of them what had happened. I made a futile attempt to take a nap but was awake again in a matter of minutes.

Now, hours later, it was quiet again. Nearly everyone had gone. My mom was now hooked up to a ventilator along with various other instruments to sustain her life and monitor her condition. Her brain scan had shown no activity for hours. A decision was made to remove her from life support in the morning. Without a shadow of a doubt, I knew she wasn't there anymore—and yet I had to talk with her. I just stood in silence, searching my heart and soul. Then the words came. They were pointed yet I didn't know what they meant. I felt a stoic determination inside of me as I said aloud, "Mom, I am going to do what you couldn't. I am going to say it."

Say what, I wondered. To whom? And yet, something inside me knew.

It would turn out to be ironic that I, out of all her children, was the one to be at her side in the last twenty-four hours of her life. I thought about that often during those hours. At one point, I even said to her that I was sure she would prefer to have any one of her other children there with her. I apologized that it was me. She couldn't respond, of course. I am not sure she was even hearing me. She was in and out of consciousness and, at one point, even slipped into a coma.

She had fought a long eight-year battle with cancer in various parts of her body and now it was attacking her brain. She would have periods of perfuse sweating and then shivering as her body would begin to turn cold. It went on like that for hours: back and forth, hot and cold. I spent those hours either hunting down blankets from reluctant nurses or pulling the blankets off her and wiping her body down from the sweat. Every surface of that room, from the floor to open shelving, was covered with used crumbled paper towels. As I cared for her, I talked with her, assuring her that she had fought long enough, telling her that it was okay to leave, telling her that we loved her. I meant it. It was time.

I prayed that God would take her so that she could finally be at peace. At peace not only from the disease of cancer, but at peace from all the hurt, regret, and betrayal she endured during her marriage. It was a marriage filled with violence of all kinds, from bruises to items being broken, to her and her children being locked out of the house, to being abandoned on a city street in a car that she didn't know how to drive, to being yelled at, to suffering through silent staring contests between her and my dad that lasted for days even to the dreaded flowers that somehow were supposed to be sufficient to say "I am sorry." Until the next time, that is!

None of what began happening after her death could have happened while she was still alive. It would have been cruel to her. I am convinced that the timing of her death was God's way of showing mercy on her. She deserved His mercy. If anyone deserved His mercy, she did.

Her death brought new life to our family. Her death ushered in the end of secrets. A new era had begun for our family: an era of truth and consequence, an era of freedom.

In her death, Dad had now become vulnerable to us.

The Soul's Fight

~ Remembering ~

A few months after my mom's death in June 1991, I moved to Hawaii. I was all of twenty-four years old and officially starting my career as an elementary school teacher at a Christian school associated with Youth With A Mission.

Hawaii is bathed in endless beauty from pristine beaches, crystal clear waters, and majestic, thundering waterfalls to rugged towering cliffs, rich verdant hills, and magma spewing volcanoes. Hawaii exudes a sense of peace and love wherever you go. Blessed with a geographical, visual, and sensual beauty beyond compare, I do believe that the natives of Hawaii have a special calling from God to offer healing and restoration to all who come to their land.

However, that isn't what drew me to Hawaii. No. What drew me to Hawaii was the distance from home. I needed the distance from family. I needed the distance from anything remotely familiar. I needed the separation to come to terms with family secrets. I needed the alone-ness to ponder the haunting words that I had spoken to my mom on her death bed.

There was now a strong stirring in my spirit. A storm was brewing inside of me. I was conflicted. I instinctively knew the cost involved. I knew the pain and discomfort that would come, not only for me, but also for my family. I knew that I was embarking on an uncertain journey with an unpredictable outcome. It was a journey that would require me to forgive a person that had hurt me so deeply that it was easier to literally not remember what had happened.

But as I would soon discover, God's love for me was so deep, so wide, so encompassing, that He wasn't content to leave me broken. I am so very thankful for that now. However, to move from brokenness to wholeness, I would have to remember what caused my brokenness in the first place.

For the next several months, cracks and fissures began to form between my conscious and unconscious realms. The cracks and fissures allowed bits and pieces of memories that had long since been suppressed to seep through. They unrelentingly erupted in my mind. The memories were often cloaked in fog, providing only a hint of what had happened. They were calling to me, gently urging me forward to reveal more of my hidden past. A fierce war began within me as horrible images of my past began to flash through my mind. I attempted to ignore the memories, turning away from them in disgust and disbelief, thinking that they couldn't possibly be true. But, at the same time, I knew them to be true. There was an undeniable familiarity with these haunting memories that confirmed the reality of my past.

In November of 1991, in one final desperate measure towards keeping the memories at bay, I suffered three grand mal seizures within one ten-hour period. In one of these seizures, I sustained a serious concussion. Awaking from this trauma, I found that I had succeeded in not only ridding myself of the horrible images, but also of people's names, places, important events, and even where I lived. Amnesia had gripped my mind. As I began to recover, I had to start a list of people's names as they visited me so I would remember them later. I would often review my list as if studying for a test.

Slowly, through the next couple of months, my memory began to return, piece by piece. During this time, I had to rely on friends that had been in my life for only three or four months prior to my seizures, concussion, and amnesia. They cared for me, checked in on me and helped me with everything that I needed. However, along with the returning memories came the horrible images of my past. Not even amnesia could prevent the truth from surfacing now. I knew there was nothing else I could do to ignore my past any longer.

The Soul's Fight

~ Assurance ~

Nearly six months after the trauma of the seizures, I was still fighting to keep my past in the shadows. It was April of 1992, and I had just completed another day of teaching my fourth-grade class in beautiful Kona, Hawaii. I walked out to the fenced boundary of the school and gazed out over the glistening ocean with tears streaming down my face. I had finally come to the realization that there was nothing else I could do to avoid the truth of my past. But before I fully surrendered to God, I had an especially important question for Him.

"God," I cried, "are YOU going to be able to handle it?"

I asked Him that because what I was about to acknowledge was so huge in my mind that I wasn't completely sure which was bigger, my memories or God. I knew that I couldn't handle this on my own. And I didn't know how my family would respond. What I needed to know with confidence was that God Himself would be there for me. That He would not abandon me. I needed reassurance. I also knew that once I stepped into this, there was no turning back.

So once again I cried, "God, are YOU going to be able to handle this?"

Without hesitation and with marked gentleness He said, *"Josee, do you see that ocean in front of you?"*

"Yes, Lord."

"Do you realize how very wide and encompassing that ocean is? Do you realize that the ocean stretches thousands of miles in one direction towards mainland USA and in the other direction

it stretches thousands of miles towards Japan and Asia? Do you realize how truly vast this ocean is? It stretches from the North Pole all the way past the continents of the world to the South Pole. And Josee, do you realize that the ocean is so deep that as strong as the sun's rays are, they can't reach the bottom?"

He paused as I took in the visual that He painted for me. He needed to alter my perspective.

With great tenderness He slowly said, *"Josee, do you think that just possibly – now remember how wide, deep, and vast this ocean is – do you think that just possibly, if you were to dump all of your emotion, pain, hurt, and memories into the sea, that the ocean would be able to contain it all?"*

With a deep breath and tears in my eyes, I said "Well, yes, I suppose so."

He was quiet for a bit as I processed it all, then He said in a firm whisper that filled my very being *"Then don't you think that I can handle it?"*

Wiping the tears from my face, I smiled and said, "Yes, Lord, you can!"

It was then that my heart finally surrendered.

~ The Flood ~

During the late morning of the next day, I went to a friend's house to ask her to silently pray over me. I immediately left once she finished praying. I returned to my friend's house a week later, knowing that I had to follow through. We sat together at her table, but I turned my back to her. I couldn't face her. After an awkward silence, barely a whisper, I asked her, "Do you remember when you prayed over me?"

She replied very simply, "Yes."

"Did the Lord show you what it was I need to remember?"

"Yes," she said again.

Silence. With my heart pounding inside of me and my brain telling my legs to stand up and leave RIGHT NOW, my spirit fought to stay. I took a deep breath and tentatively asked, "Does it have to do with my dad?"

"Yes," was her response.

My mouth found it difficult to ask the final question. This was a decisive moment. I spoke softly. "Did he do something he wasn't supposed to do?" I took a deep breath, not really wanting to hear her response.

She answered, "Yes, Josee, he did."

With that final "yes," the memories of my dad sexually abusing me flooded my mind with such a force that it actually hurt, as if the breath had been knocked out of me.

Harsh emotions that I had never known before gripped my heart. I sobbed and wailed violently. The sobbing and wailing came from the very depth of my soul and continued over many hours.

Waves of intense hurt, fierce anger, outrage, confusion, devastation, guilt, shame, fear, and betrayal consumed me. Questions raced through my mind: *Why would he do something like this? How could he do this to his little girl? What had I done that had been so bad to deserve something like this?*

Hours later, as I slowly quieted down, my friend put her hand on my back and began to silently pray over me again. I started fighting the next wave of memories that were claiming my mind, but my strength was gone. With deep anguish and bewilderment, it was then that I realized that within that incestuous relationship my dad had gotten me pregnant, and my mom had taken me for an abortion. Once again, the sobbing and guttural sounds arose from deep within, consuming me for hours more. It was now late in the evening, and I was physically and emotionally spent. I returned home and immediately fell into a deep sleep.

See Appendix B for more information on sexual abuse and Appendix C for more on abortion.

~ I Said It ~

The next morning, I awoke, totally drained and exhausted. My mind was still reeling with memories and racing with a thousand thoughts. I was overwhelmed to the point of feeling paralyzed. I couldn't think straight. I was in a daze. My friend stopped by to check on me: to make sure that I was still alive, eating, and taking care of myself. As we spoke, I began to ponder whether to contact my siblings about this. I knew that this phone call would change everything in our family. I once again felt conflicted. What's the right thing to do? Is it merciful to them to say nothing and address this on my own? Or do I have a responsibility to share this with them? Would they want to know? Would they even believe me? Would they hate me and think I was crazy? Would they tell Dad I talked about it? What would his reaction be? Would he hurt me somehow? There was a lot at stake.

However, by late afternoon, I felt very strongly that I should call them. I wasn't sure why, but I knew this had to happen. I called my sister, half hoping she would not answer. But it was not to be. She answered the phone. I suggested that she sit down as I had something to tell her, something that we needed to talk about. I struggled to form the words and stumbled over them repeatedly, not making any sense. So, I took a deep breath and started over. Slowly the words began to form.

"You need to know that Dad sexually abused me for many years. He got me pregnant. Mom took me for an abortion."

There was a momentary silence as she struggled to comprehend what I had said. But once she processed my words, she was incredibly supportive. She said she believed me and would stand by me in any decision that I made. We talked for a while, sharing many tears. She asked if I wanted her to make the other calls for me to our siblings. I agreed. I wasn't up to the task. That one phone call was completely and totally exhausting!

By the next day I had heard from all my siblings. Overall, they expressed their sadness for me as well as their support. It was good to hear from them and I felt relieved to know that they would be there for me. This was going to be a long journey.

After I had hung up with the last phone call that day, I felt relieved that this part was done, but also a bit uncertain of what was ahead. My mind returned to what I had said to my mom in the hospital as she lay there hooked up to the ventilator. It was at that moment that I fully knew and understood those words for the very first time. Sitting all alone, I spoke aloud, "Mom, I said it. I said it! It is no longer a secret!"

~ Confronting Him ~

Within a few short weeks of telling the secret to my siblings, I decided to confront my dad. Due to being in Hawaii, far from home, this was through a phone call. It didn't go well. He ranted, asking how I could possibly accuse him of such terrible things, claiming that he had never hurt me and showing disbelief that I could possibly say anything like this. I responded truthfully and confidently, stating, "The only thing I have to say is, Dad, you sexually abused me. You know what you did." Without saying another word, he hung up the phone.

I took a deep breath. I sat without moving for several minutes as I allowed the realization of what had just happened to wash over and through me. Slowly I broke into a smile. I looked at my friend, who was with me for moral support, and I actually cheered! I had finally done it! By the grace of God, I had faced the most powerful person in my life. I had faced the giant! Things were now on my terms!

I was amazed at how quickly the nature of a relationship could change. Prior to the phone call, I was always frightened of my dad. I was timid and did whatever he said I should do. Standing up to him was not a frequent occurrence. In anticipation of that fateful phone call, I was scared and nervous. I wasn't certain what I would say or how I would say it, but I knew that something had to be said. It was most definitely a defining moment in my life.

The secrets were now out. I had found my voice. And in finding my voice, his reign over me had been displaced, never to return. *Placing responsibility where it rightly belongs is a powerful choice to make as it assigns accountability to the proper person.* I was released from this false burden and finally set free to embark on my journey towards healing and restoration.

But to walk this journey, I had to completely separate from my dad. That phone call was the last call or contact I would have with my dad for the next six years. Those six years were dedicated to healing. Much like a wounded animal hides away to tend to its wounds, I had to focus on healing. I needed to tend to my wounds.

~ Torment ~

Of all the memories of abuse and violence, the reality of the abortion was the worst. It would prove to be my hardest battle I would have to fight as I learned how to forgive myself.

It took place in the summer of 1982, right before my sophomore year of high school. I remember being in the abortion clinic, lying on the table while the doctor and nurses prepared for what was about to happen next. I remember feeling so confused, not understanding what was happening or how it was that I ended up here. I remember needing my mom to be with me and feeling lonely and scared without her. Then she walked in, and a sense of relief immediately washed over me. I was beyond grateful to see her and have her in the room with me. However, that sense of relief vanished just as quickly as I watched her walk out of the room less than a minute later, leaving me alone to face what I did not – *could not* – understand.

The sense of abandonment that I felt in that moment drove a huge wedge into the very heart and soul of our relationship that would prove to be an impasse until the day that she died. I was convinced that my mom didn't love me. If she did, she would have stayed in the room with me during the abortion. If she genuinely loved me, she would have prevented the abuse in the first place. She would have left my dad. She would have gotten help and kept us safe. *Isn't that what families do for one another? "Family" is supposed to be there for one another when they are needed, no matter what, right?* But in our family, none of it was ever talked about or even recognized: not sexual abuse, not the physical violence, and most importantly, not the abortion. There was only a deafening silence throughout the years. I was filled with intense anger towards my mom.

My mom's lack of protection over me and my siblings was a betrayal that would prove to be worse than the abuse itself. As repulsive as it is to create an abusive dynamic within your own home towards your own wife and children, the perception of "allowing it to happen" is often a thousand times worse in the eyes of the victim. For in "allowing it to happen," the child is wounded to the core as he or she begins to believe it is his or her fault. The child tends to take on the blame and to suffer with guilt.

When my mom walked out of the room at the abortion clinic that day, I effectively lost my mom. The hurt she caused by doing that was just too deep to bear.

As we drove home that day, I turned my body towards the passenger's side window with my back towards her. As I numbly watched the scenery flash by, I remember wondering if my baby was a boy or a girl and what he or she would have looked like. And then, as in a whisper, a name filled my mind: *Todd Jacob.*

As with all my other traumatic memories, the abortion was filed away deep in my subconscious, not to be remembered until many years later. However, the name *Todd Jacob*, stayed with me. I didn't know why this name popped into my mind from time to time. *Who was he? What did it mean? Where did it come from?* I remember asking my siblings and friends if they knew anyone by the name of Todd Jacob. They didn't of course, but that is how real the name was to me.

The aftermath of the abortion consisted of deep-seated guilt, shame, anger, resentment, shock, and disbelief. However, since I had suppressed the memory of the abortion, these emotions had no context. Though memories can be suppressed, it is difficult to bury emotions. Emotions always find a way of expressing themselves. For me, these emotions took the form of two recurring horrific nightmares that continued to haunt me until my memories had been restored and my emotions could be fully expressed.

The first of these two nightmares took place in a car, where I was a passenger and my mom was driving. My view in this nightmare was a close-up from inside the car. As my mom was driving, she saw a man she recognized walking across the road. But instead of slowing down or stopping, she put her foot hard on the gas pedal and with her entire body forced the car right into him. I was yelling "STOP! STOP! STOP!" but she ignored my pleas. As the car hit the man, his body flew up then crashed onto the road. She sped up again and just kept on driving without saying a word.

As soon as the dream was over, it would begin again, over, and over throughout the night. That dream haunted me and riddled me with guilt. There was a part of me that couldn't fully suppress the guilt of the abortion even though the memory was tucked away. Even though in the dream it was obvious that I wasn't the driver, it would take me a long time to realize that. I had no control over the car. I had no control over whether the person had been hit or not. I was hauntingly—tragically—just along for the ride.

The same was, I would discover, also true of my abortion. I came to realize, through counseling, that I wasn't responsible for the pregnancy or the abortion. I had no control over what happened. But for many years, those simple truths eluded me and, as a result, deep heartfelt shame consumed me.

In the second reoccurring nightmare, I would be walking down the stairs in our home to the basement with my sisters, where my dad had his business. My sisters bounded down the steps laughing and giggling. As I was descending the stairs, there was a certain section of the wall on my right where I heard a voice cry out:

> *"Why are you doing this to me?"*
> Startled, I said, "What? Who are you?"
> The voice responded, *"You know who I am."*
> "No, I don't. How could I know?"
> *"You know,"* it firmly and loudly stated.
> "How did you get into the wall?" I asked.
> *"You put me here."*
> And then it would start again. "Why are you doing this to me?"

This nightmare, like the first one, haunted me and repeatedly filled me with horror.

Though at the time I did not understand who was speaking to me, calling me, and traumatizing me, I now understand that the "voice" represents my guilt and shame over aborting Todd Jacob. Though the memories of sexual abuse and abortion were safely tucked away in the dark recesses of my mind, I was not free from their emotional impact. So along with a deep sense of guilt, whose source I could never quite pinpoint, the nightmares, anger towards my mom, feeling unsafe, an aversion towards my dad, the name Todd Jacob, and the frequent reoccurring seizures were ever present. What I lacked was the context. I was missing the conscious memory of why these nightmares and burdens were a part of my life. I was deeply confused and disturbed by all of this.

See Appendix C for more information on abortion.

~ Physical Toll ~

My parents put all their children through a Catholic school, from first grade all the way through twelfth grade. Each of us responded differently to that experience. I am deeply thankful for it because it laid a foundation of faith in God for me that became my ray of hope throughout my childhood. I clung to God from an early age. He was everything to me. I am certain that without Him in my life during those years, I wouldn't have survived the trauma. As a result of the abuse, a real risk of physical death or permanent damage – emotionally, physically or psychologically – had loomed over me. God was my one hope that things would get better. It was my early grounding in faith, facilitated by my Catholic schooling, which provided this hope.

However, the Catholic Church and school experience had a negative impact on me as well. It instilled fear, guilt, and condemnation. It created a nearly daily routine that would play out between teachers, principal, priests, and myself. In this routine, I would pester the teachers to allow me to meet with the priest for a few minutes to confess my sins. After futilely attempting to ignore my request, the teacher would give in. Once gaining permission, I would run to the principal's office as fast as I could and beg him to allow me to meet with a priest right away.

Again, only due to my persistence did he agree. After all, how do a nun and a principal of a Catholic school deny a child the right to confess sin when that is what we were taught all the time! My sins needing confession were so small and trivial that the priest would often have a tough time holding back his laughter and taking it seriously. I, on the other hand, took it very seriously. I was convinced that I would miss heaven if I were to die with unconfessed sin in my heart.

Now take a teenager who grew up in the Catholic Church, riddled with guilt over the smallest of missteps, and put on her additional years of sexual abuse and, worse yet for a Catholic girl, an abortion, and what are the results? In my innocence and naiveté, my thinking was so twisted at the time that I viewed my sexual abuse as a form of adultery and took on the weight of all that it implied. These sins couldn't be confessed to anyone for fear for my own life.

That was the impossible burden I carried as I walked into my sophomore English class in October 1982, just a few months following the abortion. We were studying the book *The Scarlet Letter* by Nathaniel Hawthorne. The book was about condemnation of a woman who had an affair. I remember sitting there in the class feeling totally exposed; surely everyone now knew. What was I going to do? There was no escape, except to shut down and withdraw. So, shut down and withdraw I did. I didn't make it to my next class. Instead, I had a seizure in the school hallway and spent the next week in the hospital. This seizure would prove to be just the first of many to occur for several years despite taking my prescribed medications daily.

Prior to the seizure in 1982, I had only one other seizure in my life. That was when I was two years old, and it was due to a high fever. But that wasn't the cause of the seizures I experienced throughout my high school years. Both the recurrence of the seizures and their apparent unresponsiveness to at least four different anti-seizure medications confounded my neurologist. Looking for answers or confirmation of my suspicion, I have researched this myself several times. Each time, I found a lack of research to document this course of the disease.

The common course of this disease is revealed in the following research:

> *"New cases of epilepsy are most common among children, especially during the first year of life. The rate of new cases gradually declines until about age 10, and then becomes stable. After age 55 or 60, the rate starts to increase, as people develop strokes, brain tumors or Alzheimer's disease." (Schachter, 2006)*

So, not only is it unusual for an adolescent to develop epilepsy, but it is also even stranger for it to recur some thirteen years later. *"About half of the people who have one seizure without a clear cause will have another one, usually within 6 months." (Schachter, 2008)* Clearly, mine was not a typical case for a person with epilepsy. Doctors performed more tests on me than I can count. The tests gave little insight into why these seizures were occurring. Though many doctors consulted on my case, the presence of the epilepsy remained a mystery to the medical establishment.

Following graduation from high school in 1985, I didn't have any other seizures until November 1991 when I had begun fighting back the memories that were trying to surface. I do believe with all my heart, in my case, that the seizures were caused by trauma resulting from the years of sexual abuse and the abortion that I had endured, to say nothing of the unbearable guilt I shouldered because of that abuse. The events of my life – the incest, estrangement from my mother, and the secret abortion – couldn't be reconciled with the "Catholic" reality that I was immersed in every day at school. I was devastated by the events of my life and so overwhelmed by the trauma of it all that I literally shut down: physically, emotionally, and mentally.

Due to the violent nature of my home environment and the constant worry, stress and anxiety that clouded my mind, it was difficult for me to focus on schoolwork. Consequently, my grades were all over the place. After the abortion, it became even worse. Though I loved being at school, since it provided a safe refuge from home, focusing on my studies was another matter. Teachers expressed exasperation with my inability to grasp certain concepts.

Parent-Teacher Conferences yielded little help to me. Teachers became suspicious of what I was going through as they noticed a decline in my grades, a change in my moods, my increased tendency to withdraw from friends and the recurrence of seizures that had no known medical cause. They even checked my locker on a regular basis for drugs and alcohol, to no avail. I was on their radar, but they had no idea what was going on with me or how to help me.

At this point in my family's history, all my older siblings were off to college. Dad had long been working from home and, for the first time ever, my mom had started working outside the home. I was depressed and felt completely alone and vulnerable. Being at home after school with only my dad, until Mom came home from work, left me feeling trapped. Those few hours were torture for me as I tried to stay away from him for as long as I could. I started filling my life with jobs and volunteering just so I wouldn't have to go home. On more than one occasion, I even purposely took the wrong school bus home just to shorten my time at home with my dad.

My anger towards my mom only increased during that time. When she chose to go to work for the first time since being married, it was as if she was deserting and abandoning me all over again. My anger was more intense than any emotion I had ever felt. Wasn't she supposed to care for me? *Wasn't she supposed to be there for me? Wasn't she supposed to create a safe place for me, to nurture me, and provide for me? Why had she stayed home with my siblings, but left me home alone? After the abortion, how could she not know that I needed her protection from my dad?*

My anger towards my mom showed itself often. I was disrespectful, resentful, and bitter. It alienated us. I was consumed by my anger towards her. My heart had no room or desire to care about what she was going through.

In 1983, less than a year after my abortion, my mom discovered she had uterine cancer. It was found because of a medical evaluation following a car accident that had totaled her car. If it hadn't been for the accident, it could easily have been too late by the time the cancer was found. *"Stress, different researchers now suggest, can trigger a variety of ailments – from arthritis, headaches, herpes, high blood pressure, gastrointestinal problems, and insomnia, to heart disease, AIDS, and cancer."* (Groves, 1996) Stress is a sinister thing and trauma is even worse.

I believe my mom's sense of guilt over not protecting her children was so profound that it literally made her sick. *"Stress triggers a primitive fight-or-flight response that increases heart and breathing rates, pumps extra adrenaline into the blood, and dilates the eyes to bring in more light. The response helps humans survive danger, but chronic stress is tough on the nerves and the immune system, especially if the response is internalized instead of expressed."* (Groves, 1996)

There is an abundance of scientific research which speaks to how interlinked our bodies are with our soul, mind, and spirit. I don't think that either the location of the cancer in her body or the timing of her cancer was a coincidence, just as I don't think the timing or reoccurrence of my seizures was a coincidence. We were both suffering from internal turmoil over the abortion and abuse. We both responded to these horrific life events through physical illness. I want to be clear that I don't believe either of our illnesses were a result of God punishing us. Rather, I believe it was an organic response to severe trauma.

~ The Soul's Fight ~

Up until the time of remembering the abuse and making it known to my family, my soul was held captive. It was filled with hurt and wounds and had become ferociously protective and guarded. There was no obvious way of taking care of these wounds, so they continued to bleed and fester. There was no real path set before me. I had spent a lot of energy hiding my wounds and secrets away, to the very depths of my being, where no one could access them – not even me. Now the memories had found their way to freedom. What would be next?

I was about to gain a glimpse into the value of my soul.

Within a month of remembering all these memories, a fight began for my soul. It was a fight for freedom. The fight was not only with me, but with Satan and God as well. It was through this fight that motives and plans were revealed. It was through this fight that I was shown the most treasured part of our being: the soul.

The soul is where our very essence lies. It is where our potential awaits to be tapped into. It is where our purpose is stored until the day that we realize we are not our own. We were created by God for a reason and for a purpose. That purpose is never just for ourselves, but it is intended for those around us as well. By tiny ripple or mighty wave, our purpose is intended to affect the world. We all suffer when that purpose remains unfulfilled. But we are all blessed each time it is allowed to reveal itself.

Our soul is what communes with God. It is the part of us that bonds with family and friends. We all face influences in our life that pollute our souls with distractions or tragedies. The world we live in lures us into things that seem good and pleasurable, but inevitably these things have a sting hidden within. We all have our struggles, whether it is substance abuse, gambling, love of money, seeking the perfect image, prestige, status, wanting to be noticed by our peers or countless others. They may all be packaged differently, but their sting is the same.

Why would Satan, God and even we ourselves go to so much trouble to influence the soul if it wasn't worth anything? Satan wouldn't attempt to derail us and seek to destroy us if our soul was worth nothing. God wouldn't have sent His only Son to die for your soul if it was worth nothing. Neither of them would have bothered.

Whenever I hear of a tragedy in a person's life, my first thought is to pray for the person's soul and to pray for God the Redeemer to bring good from the tragedy, for a person's soul is in the balance. You see, a tragedy holds both the potential to turn a person from their purpose or to turn them towards it. Make no mistake; there are always eternal ramifications involved.

I was at that point myself once the memories began to surface. I could allow the memories to destroy me or I could allow them to propel me towards my God-created purpose. I had a choice to make. On one hand I could choose to bury these memories again, say nothing, and continue to live out my "woundedness." Or, on the other hand, I could choose to face the memories and all that they held in store. Both choices would require determination; both would be painful. Neither offered any promises of a bright future.

There was one big difference in the two choices that lay before me: one held destruction and the other held hope. Weighing in the balance was the condition of my very soul. Many people go through life with a damaged soul. Relationships barely alive, discontent in most if not all areas of life, unfulfilled potential, dreams long forgotten, and living from one day to another without much to distinguish them. It wreaks of a complete lack of purpose. But we are created with purpose. When that purpose is ignored, something inside of our soul dies. *Our purpose is designed to fulfill us while we positively impact others around us.* Our purpose, when discovered and expressed, fills us with joy. When we are engaged in that purpose, it feels like nothing else in the world.

Many times, our purpose is veiled or not realized due to unresolved issues, unspoken conflict, living to please others, being disconnected from others, guilt, anger, bitterness, or unforgiveness, to mention only a few. These negative conditions of the heart clog our hearts and souls and prevent us from being the person God created us to be. In those moments, in those circumstances, a fight for your soul is waging within you whether you are aware of it or not. It is a fight which reverberates from the depth of your being. It is a fight against all those justifications that keep us ensnared, resulting in broken relationships. It is a fight to be set free. The soul knows when it is imprisoned, and it fights against it for freedom – for release – because without freedom there is only death.

So, I had a choice to make. Would I continue to try to bury my memories, or would I face them? Would I live with the memories buried inside and die, or would I fight for my soul?

Do not minimize the worth of your soul. It holds eternal value. Consider what God did to purchase the freedom of every soul He created. He sacrificed His only Son so that we might be free from the effects of sin. Jesus' love for every person is unyielding; He pursues each of us from the moment of our first breath to our last. He cries out to us. He makes Himself known and offers us the ultimate gift: salvation from all that aims to destroy us. He offers us Himself. He holds the power to take the hurts and wounds of our lives and turn them into beauty. He holds the power to turn our sorrow into joy. He holds the power to turn burdens into delight. He does this with amazing joy in His heart towards the one that says "Yes" to Him. Please know this: your soul is priceless.*

Satan knows this as well. He knows this better than we do. He understands the worth of one soul and is determined to destroy it in any way he can. It might be a dramatic destruction such as murder, violence, or abuse. Or it could be subtle erosion of the soul through pointed hurtful words, or through being demeaned, ignored, disregarded, or devalued. The method doesn't matter to Satan, his only concern is the outcome. He is willing to do absolutely anything to steal your soul from you.

Proverbs 4:23 encourages us to *"Above all else, guard your heart, for everything you do flows from it"* (NIV). Wow! Those are strong words. What we allow to reside within our hearts or souls will influence the decisions and the course of our lives. With every decision made, we either walk further away from the purpose of our lives or we walk closer to it.

(See Appendix A for a prayer of salvation)

Like many, I had a fair amount of "head knowledge." But before the following encounter, I didn't fully realize the depth of value that lies within a soul. Now I know! I hope and pray that through hearing of this experience, you will begin to realize your soul's value as well.

Within a month after most of my memories had surfaced, I had an encounter with Satan. There is a continual battle being fought for our souls, whether we realize it or not. Some encounters are subtle, while others are more dramatic. This encounter, for me, was on the dramatic side. I was in my bedroom, writing in my journal when I suddenly became aware of a presence in my room. I looked around but couldn't see anyone. But the feeling of this presence became stronger, sending chills down my back. I realized this wasn't a person and it wasn't God, for with the awareness of this presence came a sense of evil. All my senses were on high alert. I put down my pen and journal and turned my attention to what I could now make out as a form standing a few feet from the side of my bed. There were no identifiable features, just a form. But it was huge and intimidating.

The room seemed to darken, and it was getting hard to breathe. I sensed a sinister laugh coming from this form. I instinctively cried out, "No! No!" I sensed the laugh again. Knowing this was not a battle of flesh and blood, but a spiritual one, I fell to my knees and cried out the name, "Jesus." I cried out for my freedom. I made defining statements such as "I will not live in bondage," "I will not take the burden on again," "I receive Jesus' healing," and "I claim my freedom in Him."

I cried out, I prayed, and I sweated. The battle was on. As in any battle, you can sense who is winning at any given moment.

This battle swayed back and forth, in rhythm with my faith in God to deliver me. I was strong one moment, weak the next. I cried out, I gave in, I cried out, I gave in. The battle continued.

I had a decision to make. Which would be easier? Living in bondage or fighting for my freedom? I sensed the laugh again. This renewed my determination. My faith in God was my strength. This experience lasted for what seemed like hours; back and forth. Then finally, just as suddenly as the presence had arrived, it was gone. I had been released. I was exhausted and dripping in sweat. I pulled myself up from the floor and fell onto the bed, falling immediately into a deep restorative sleep. When I awoke, I felt renewed and light. I thanked God, reflected on the experience, and wrote the following poem.

The Soul's Fight

A word, A thought, A feeling
A beam of light in the darkest corner of the heart.
The Truth!

>With the light the darkness was threatened.
>The fight began!

The fight for freedom. The fight for wholeness.
The fight to be set free!

>The chains were rattled. The bondage was pierced.
>The heart was shaken.
>Satan declared war!

The cry was louder. The prayer was stronger.
The knees were sturdy.
The Angels came!

>The soul was strengthened. The spirit was lifted.
>The heart surrendered.
>The counter-attacked released!

The cry was silenced. The prayer was choked.
The knees were wobbly.
Darkness consumed!

>The Hand reached out. The warriors fought.
>The spirit was revived.
>The Light prevailed!

Sight was restored. The bondage was lifted.
The heart rejoiced!
God's character was proven!
Great is His Faithfulness!

>The chains were broken. The war had been won.
>The soul and spirit had been set free.
>He whom the Lord sets free is free indeed!

A word. A thought. A feeling. Light!
>The Truth!

At the very moment that I am writing this, tears are streaming down my face. They are tears of thankfulness to my God who loves me so very much that He is willing to fight for me! In the hour of my need, He came. This experience spoke volumes for me. It spoke of Satan's desire to destroy by smothering the soul with a blanket of darkness. Satan was threatened when my memories returned, dispelling his darkness with the Light of Truth.

Satan had been content with my bondage. He knew that as long as I walked in bondage, I would not be able to fulfill God's purpose for my life. He knew that I was God's child, and he was threatened as I neared my purpose. For in walking the journey of healing, I was getting closer to being able to speak into other people's lives about the Redeemer! Satan wasn't willing to let go of his power over me. So, he came to ensure I kept walking in bondage. In bondage, I wouldn't be effective in God's purpose and therefore wouldn't be any threat to the kingdom of darkness.

This experience also spoke to me of God's relentless love and desire to see His people free. He shows up every time war is declared on one of His own. God came and fought for me. He fought for my freedom. He fought for the bondage to lose its power. He fought so that I would be able to walk into His purpose for me. He fought to set me free. He fought to set me on a path of healing, a path of forgiveness, a path that would lead to His ordained purpose.

But notice that I also fought! That is important. It didn't happen that once Satan and God showed up in my bedroom, I just sat back and watched. No. I was an active participant in this battle. I fought a spiritual battle with spiritual weapons:

prayer and scripture. If I had chosen not to participate in this battle, then I would have lost. I had to cry out from the depths of my being. And with every cry I was making a choice: a choice to walk this path of healing. Healing doesn't just sneak up on you one day. It doesn't just happen. Healing is something you must set your eyes and heart on and fight for, and never accept defeat. It is the Soul's Fight.

Do you see how valuable your soul is? It is priceless!

SECTION TWO
The Journey Toward Forgiveness

The Soul's Fight

Looking Out the Window

I look out the window
I see the snow flurries coming down.
I see the happy faces of the children
I long to join them, run with them, laugh with them.
I long to feel the white, wet snow against my boot.
I long to form a single snowball within my hands.
I long to make a snowman, to go sleighing.

But I cannot join the children in the snow.
Because I cannot walk.
I am paralyzed
But that is okay because I can do things they cannot.
And perhaps I will learn to walk
and join the happy faces in the snow.

The Soul's Fight

~ The Healing Process ~

The healing process is different for everyone. It looks different. It feels different. It has different twists and turns, different rhythms, different themes, and different timing. All healing is sacred for it comes from the hand of God. Healing is a complex process with no straight paths or even clear direction. It's messy to say the least. It's painful. So, why go through it?

Many people don't.

They avoid the healing process at all costs. The thing is, though, avoiding pain is also painful. It typically catches up with you at some point. It is evident through a trail of broken relationships, lost jobs, financial ruin, addictions, and alienations. These troubles only compound the original source of pain.

So, the choice is either you live with your pain for the rest of your life, or you face it, feel it, wrestle with it and make changes in your life and relationships. It takes a great amount of courage to face pain. I admire anyone who is brave enough to say with a deep breath and body braced, "Okay, bring it on! Let's do this." I know from experience that it is worth every bit of pain to find peace from the troubles within.

The healing process can vary from a completely solitary process to one that is walked with a group of people supporting you along the way. It can be loud and all consuming, or quiet and subtle. It can involve making amends to those you have hurt or forgiving someone who hurt you. It can be done in a moment, or it may take years to complete. It can be active and creative, or simple yet profound. It can be a simple word spoken at the right time or can require seeking someone out. It can revolve around one key person in your life or numerous people. It can be a piece of art that awakens the spirit or a sunset on a quiet stretch of beach. It can involve all the senses working together in harmony for the first time in your life after one or two senses have been silenced by a trauma or hurt. It can be finding your voice after years of only pleasing others. It can be learning how to set a boundary in your life and saying "no" for the very first time.

Whatever your journey will include, I am certain of these few things: it will have ups and downs, it will be difficult, it will require sheer determination, it will go against your emotions and thinking at times, it will involve tears, screams and outrage, it will cause chaos in your life for a while and even in the lives of those who love you, it will have moments of failure and stumbles, and it will bring you to the depths of your soul. I am also certain about this, though: it is worth every bit of that and more.

On the other hand, all this pain will be forgotten as you stand marveling at the beauty that resides within you and become aware of a deep well of confidence that is alive within you. Intact relationships will begin to fill your life, health will take up residence, and a smile that you just can't seem to wipe away will form on your face. It was true for me, and it has been true for so many others that I have the pleasure of knowing! It is the most fabulous journey I have ever been on!

The first two years of my journey were rather rocky as I was deeply depressed, not eating, not sleeping, and often crying uncontrollably. I was at times consumed with the desire to numb the pain and to forget the memories. In pursuit of that, I would often find myself in my car circling liquor stores, feeling conflicted inside. Though I had never drank any kind of alcohol, the desire to drink was immensely strong during that time in my life. It was precisely the strength of that desire that scared me and caused me to feel out of control. That was not what I wanted! I had been out of control throughout my childhood, attempting to survive, even just one day at a time. Now, I was conflicted with the desire to numb the pain and the need to maintain control. There were times though that I would circle the block up to ten times before finally just driving away.

I'm not at all sure what kept me from walking into the liquor store besides the fear of what it would do to me. I was certain it would destroy me, and I wasn't sure at all how I would find my way back. I remember the battle in my mind as I circled the block repeatedly. I remember the torment. I remember screaming from the emotional pain. No words, just screaming. I remember not being sure I was capable of enduring any more pain. The war was on inside of me.

I knew if I drank it would only make my mess worse, and it was already more than I could bear. Each time I arrived home, I busied myself with projects or activities to keep my mind off the alcohol until the urge passed. If the urge was too strong, I would go to a friend's house to ensure I didn't drink. I kept a list of things to do when I felt the urge so I had something physical to pull out and look at. Relying on my mind while in that state was not a dependable option, as my mind was locked in what seemed to be a constant battle. I needed something removed from that battle to guide me. So, when the urges returned, this plan seemed effective.

This urge is abundantly rare at this point, but when it comes, I remind myself that it is like poison to my body and only holds destruction for me. To date, I have never given into the urge. I have on occasion sipped champagne or some wine on a special occasion with friends. Typically, I don't even finish half a glass and I never consume it if the urge to drink is present or has recently returned. I don't know the struggle of attempting to live a sober life after years and even decades of alcoholism. I didn't have to face that. But I do know the struggle to deny the urge to drink; it is alluring and deceptive. I am grateful that it is a battle that I don't have to fight on my own.

As a Licensed Marriage and Family Therapist, I know that the struggle with addiction is powerful. In no way do I think I am any better than anyone who has struggled with this issue in a deeper way than I have. If anything, I know it could easily have been me. I have seen and worked with many addicts and their families; there is nothing easy about it. Everyone involved is deeply impacted by addiction and it often consumes decades of a person's and their family's life before recovery takes place, if at all.

What I have experienced is but a glimpse of the grip it has on many lives. If this is an issue you struggle with, I urge you to seek professional support. There are so many programs available with many different approaches. Choose carefully to find what fits best for you. If you are a family member or friend of a person who struggles with an addiction, numerous places offer professional support for you as well.

See Appendix D for more information on addictions.

During the first two years of my journey of healing, my desire to live was pretty low. There was one point at which I planned to end my life. It seemed like my only alternative to the unbearable pain. I waited for the family I lived with at the time to leave for the night. I planned to wait about ten minutes after they left to avoid them returning for some unforeseen reason and interrupt me. I lay down in my bed with everything ready and with nothing left to do but wait. I was alert, focused and resolute. There wasn't a doubt in my mind that I wanted to die. I was willing to see it through.

But the next thing I knew, it was the morning of the next day. I awoke with disbelief and cried out, "Why?" I slammed my fists against the wall. I couldn't believe it. How did this happen? I didn't want to be alive. I couldn't go on. There was nothing to live for. There was only more pain and misery.

At a loss of what to do next, I turned to the only source of strength I knew, my faith in God. I began to pray. While praying, I became certain that it was God who had put me to sleep that night to spare my life. There could be no other explanation.

As I sat there, I was reminded of the moment when I stood facing the ocean and God assured me that He could handle it. I cried out "I can't handle it. It's too much. It's too painful." I needed to get out of my own head. I needed something outside of myself to fight this battle. I turned on some Christian music and for the next three to four hours I sang along, filling my mind with truths of hope, comfort and peace. Song after song after song filled my thoughts—pushing out the negative, consuming and destructive thoughts. As each negative thought was replaced with a hopeful one, my strength returned bit by bit.

I called a friend and told her what had happened. I spent the next few days and nights with her to avoid being alone again until those thoughts lost their power. At times throughout the next three years, thoughts of ending my life would return. But I had my plan ready: play Christian music, journal, pray, spend time with a friend who knew my struggle, and work through it in counseling.

Suicide, of course, packs a very powerful blow, even if it is the struggle of unrelenting thoughts. It holds its own brand of torment for all involved. Many times, it continues knocking, consuming the person it torments. Its voice is loud, and it often deafens a person's ability to reason. It cloaks itself in a promise of peace, with no intention of keeping the promise. It is often accompanied by guilt, shame, isolation, fear, anxiety, hopelessness, and insomnia, to name a few. If this is an issue you struggle with, I urge you to seek professional support. If you are a friend of someone in this situation, the best thing you can do is to take them to a professional who is equipped and trained in this area.*

Thoughts of drinking and suicide were just two ways that my pain manifested itself. Just as healing is different for everyone, so does pain manifest itself differently. Survivors of sexual abuse may struggle with self-mutilation or "cutting," anger, impulsivity, gambling, depression, eating issues, risk-taking behaviors, promiscuity, or others. These behaviors often mask the real pain that lies beneath them. Once the real pain is addressed, these tendencies aren't needed anymore and typically cease.

See Appendix E for more information on suicide

Shortly after this time I met an amazing friend, a godly woman who took me under her wing. She exuded love and compassion towards me and always knew the exact right words to say to me. She was safe. I was drawn towards her and soaked in all the encouragement she gave to me. She helped me grieve and she inspired me to open my heart towards God's healing. It was her friendship that got me through the journey of healing.

Everyone needs at least one trusted person during these trying times to talk through the hurts and gain compassion and perspective. I leaned on her and looked to her for strength. I thank God for her and the influence she had in my life. I would encourage you to find that person in your life, whether that is a skilled friend, mentor, or professional therapist.

I also found that taking long drives around the Big Island of Hawaii offered solace as I found quiet places looking out on the ocean. These became sacred places where I could sit quietly, or cry and scream as I poured my heart out to God. I took these trips often; they were deeply healing for me. My favorite places were the cliffs. I would sit on the ground, close my eyes, place the palm of my hands on the ground close to my body and wait for the waves to crash up against the cliffs with such force that it created a loud clap and shook the ground I sat on. It was thrilling and made me feel alive. I hung onto that feeling as I fought for life and healing. It was a fight for my soul!

Throughout my healing process, journaling and writing poems or stories became a powerful tool as well. Some of those journal entries and poems are included in this book. I filled numerous notebooks as I wrote down my thoughts and feelings. I spent many an hour journaling about the devastating effects of the abuse as well as the hope that I found in God. Journaling is a powerful tool. It can draw out words that reside within the soul. It allows a person to find his or her voice, creating clarity and insight into how a hurt, wound, or trauma has impacted his or her life.

Often, the way out is hidden within your journal entries as emotions are untangled, thoughts are identified, intentions are exposed, and the soul's hope is revealed. Emotions stubbornly reside within a person until they find a way of being expressed. Emotions may even lay dormant for decades. But often the emotions are so strong that as soon as they surface, you would think the incident that those emotions are attached to had just taken place. Journaling allows those emotions to have a life – to have a voice – making it possible for the person to also find life.

When I think of healing, I remember a time when I was teaching first grade in Hawaii. We engaged in a science project of watching the incubation and hatching process of chicken eggs. Some of the students' parents set us up with the necessary equipment and eggs. Everything was precisely monitored, from the temperature in the incubator to the temperature in the brooder that was created for the chicks after they hatched. We watched day after day. Each class would come by to ask, "Have they hatched today?" or "How much longer until they hatch?" It really became a school wide project! The day came when the chicks started to hatch. It didn't take long before the entire school knew about it, and every class took turns to come see the amazing sight as egg after egg became a baby chicken right before their eyes! It truly was amazing.

However, there was one problem: one of the eggs didn't hatch. We had moved all the baby chicks into their new home so they would stay warm and have soft bedding under their feet. But one egg remained in the incubator. I was determined to not give up on it, even when everyone else was sure it was dead. I waited an entire day and into the next evening. I stayed in the classroom into the night to see if it would hatch. A few other teachers joined me as we waited and prayed for this little chick. Finally, late in the evening, movement was detected. We were enthralled and tried to contain our excitement, as if our shrills would have disturbed the chick somehow.

The chick struggled to make its way out of the egg. It was tempting to help it, but I knew if we helped, the chick would not develop the muscles it would need to stand and walk once it was free of its shell. It needed that struggle to be strong and prepared for life. So, we agonized and cheered it on. Finally, it broke free. It was apparent that the chick was exhausted. It lay there without moving for several minutes and then struggled to stand. It wasn't doing well, and it became clear that if I placed it with all the other chicks that now had a day and a half on this chick, it would be trampled by them and likely die.

I didn't have the necessary materials to create another suitable home for this chick and it couldn't stay in the incubator. I stood there for several minutes trying to figure out what to do. I had an idea. I took a piece of cardboard and made a separate pocket of space within the brooder of the other chicks, just for this one fragile little chick. That way it would have everything it needed without being in danger of being trampled. I placed the chick in this space and watched it for some time to be sure it would be okay. Within two days it was strong, standing and walking. It could hold its own. I removed the cardboard, and it ran towards its brothers and sisters. It just needed a safe place to heal and recuperate for a little while. Soon, it was difficult to identify that chick from all the others.

For me, this is a great picture of the healing process. Healing is a struggle that is painful to go through. It is also painful for others to watch a loved one walking through it. However, just like the chick had to struggle to get out of the shell to be strong and prepared for life, so is the healing process. Healing is a "process" for that exact reason: it is the struggle that makes us strong and ready for the next step of life. This picture also speaks of a safe warm place with everything you need, but sheltered and protected from further harm, while you recover from your wounds and hurts.

It is encouraging to me that once the chick had gained its strength and was released to join the other chicks, I could no longer tell it apart from the others. The same is true for us. Once healed, your wounds and hurts will no longer be your identity. They will no longer dictate decisions, relationships, responses, or emotions. You will no longer be known by your past. You will be known by your strength.

I am certainly a much stronger person on this side of my healing than I ever was on the other side! Jesus held me in His hands, safe from the world, as He spoke healing over me. He can and will do the same for you. That is what He does. That is who He is. I pray that you can allow Him to hold you in His hands as you heal. It is the safest place in the world.

Though my healing process had many different aspects, I would say that the most significant ones were discovering the character of God, rewiring my thinking patterns, and walking the path of forgiveness. I would like to briefly talk about the first two before delving more into forgiveness.

Discovering the Character of God

We all form an image of who God is based on our life experiences. Therefore, our image of God is marred and far from the reality of who He really is. The most profound influences of how we form our understanding of God is from our parents. How they treat us becomes how we expect God to treat us. Their personality becomes God's personality, their values, His values and so on. I was no different. Since my dad was abusive, it was impossible for me to think of God as a loving Father. I avoided the name "Father" in reference to Him at all costs. I would cringe inside whenever "Father" was mentioned by someone in reference to God. This image of God needed to change. I needed to know the true character of God, but how?

The foundation for discovering the character of God began during my time with Youth With A Mission (YWAM) in Amsterdam, Holland and then in Kona, Hawaii. YWAM introduced me to experiencing God – that is, truly interacting with Him. Though I had yearned for a relationship with God from childhood, it was during my time with YWAM that I realized God wanted a relationship with me! In this realization I discovered a vibrant, living God who was no longer elusive but personal and intimately acquainted with everything that was happening in my life. I discovered a God who intimately cared how I spent my time, how I treated others, my concerns, my dreams, and so on.

Soon, I grew to expect an interactive relationship with Him in which He spoke to me, and I heard Him. It was a relationship in which I learned how to be led by Him and in which I explored the myriads of ways in which to pray to Him. I discovered a God who willingly and actively pursues each of us and I witnessed His pursuit in the lives of the people we interacted with in Amsterdam. I discovered a God of healing, a God who is gentle and precise.

One such experience with God occurred soon after arriving in Amsterdam. YWAM often sends teams on "prayer walks" in which the team walks various parts of the city and prays for the city. The team prays for the people, for God's will to be done. for a heart for the city and the community, and for salvation and healing. The walks would include the red-light district in which prostitutes would sit in house windows waiting for customers. These prayer walks occurred continually throughout my time in Amsterdam, and it was truly a tragic and deeply disturbing experience for me.

During a staff meeting a few weeks after one of these prayer walks, a guest speaker presented a message on the spiritual stronghold of sexual abuse over the city. More than forty members of the team were seated in a circle in a large room. I was seated on the opposite side of the circle from the speaker. Though the circle was large, I felt he was speaking only to me. I began to feel like the room was getting smaller and smaller. I felt sick to my stomach and became feverish. It was becoming hard for me to breathe. I had no idea what was going on or why I was reacting this way. I only knew I had to get out of the room. Something had jolted my core, and I was struggling to maintain my composure. Without even seeing it coming, an arrow had pierced my armor and, just like that, the first step towards bringing light to the darkness had taken place.

This is an illustration of a Living God who is gentle and yet precise in His pursuit of His people.

Despite having no remembrance of what I had lived through as a child and therefore no desire to pursue healing, God knew everything. He began His work in me to bring those memories to the surface. This was the first arrow to penetrate the steel armor used to guard me from unknown trauma. This experience in itself did not bring the memories to light immediately. I remained in the dark. However, when I did remember some two years later, I recalled this moment vividly and recognized God's hand in my life. I stood amazed and began to understand this astounding display of love, care, concern, and compassion. He made the first move. By doing so, He displayed His broken heart for my brokenness. He also expressed His desire to bring healing to my soul.

A few months later, still in Amsterdam with YWAM, I encountered another facet of the Living God. This took the form of tenderness.

Flowers are inexpensive and incredibly beautiful in Amsterdam. They were always abundant, filling the city with vivid color and indescribable fragrances. It was rare to go to someone's home and not see fresh flowers. So, one day I brought tulips home for my bedroom with great anticipation of how those tulips would brighten up my room. However, I was soon perplexed. The flowers wouldn't open; they remained tight in buds. For many mornings I would wake up hoping that they had bloomed during the night. Nothing; they just wouldn't bloom. Nearly a week had gone by and still they had not opened. Then one morning as I turned to look at them, every one of them had opened wide. I jumped out of bed, ran over to them and inhaled breath after breath of wonderful, sweet fragrance. Then I heard His still small voice say, "I take even more delight in you when you open up to me."

It was in that moment that I discovered that God woos us to Himself. I experienced a Father yearning to hear the voice of His child, to delight in what she delights in, to celebrate a simple joy with her. He became a Father who desires to spend time with His child. I was in tears. I had never experienced this kind of gentle, tender love from a father before. I hadn't expected that God would care about some simple tulips that wouldn't bloom. I didn't expect that He knew or would understand my frustration morning after morning. I really didn't expect that He had the time for such seemingly trivial things.

The Father's words brought healing to me, because with those simple words He ushered me to Himself. This touched my spirit and created a desire within me to be with Him. For once, I felt loved completely. I felt like there was nowhere that He wanted to be but with me. For the first time, I spoke words to Him that were personal instead of formal. I spoke from my heart instead of my mind. I shared desires, fears, and hopes with Him that morning. The words that He had spoken to me changed my relationship with Him forever. Never again would I approach Him from a distance. I had now experienced Him personally and simply. Though I hadn't known this kind of love from my own father, I was beginning to experience a Father's heart for his daughter. My heart was opened to His touch again.

In the months that followed, I noticed posters throughout the city of Amsterdam. I don't remember what was being advertised, but the image of the poster was compelling. At the top of the poster was the image of a rocking horse. And then at the bottom of the poster was a picture of a real horse running free. Words filled the poster, but the words eluded me at the time and are really of no importance now. It was the image that captured my attention.

Wherever I encountered this poster, I would have difficulty averting my eyes from it. Each time I saw it, it had the same effect. I seemed to be mesmerized by it. I didn't realize why – until one day as I was ascending the stairs from the subway, I saw this poster again. Since I was ascending the stairs, I only had a partial view of the poster; I could only see the rocking horse. Of course, a rocking horse is not real; its feet are bound to the wood below it and it is only a replica – a simple shell of the real thing. I stopped in my tracks as I realized, *I am the rocking horse.*

I said silently in my heart, "God, that is me, isn't it?"
"*Yes,*" He answered, "*for now.*"
"For now?" I wondered what He meant.
"*That is not my plan for you,*" He said simply.
I paused, thinking and then whispered,
"Oh, the real horse?"
"*Yes, Josee, the real horse! That is my plan for you!*"

I laughed as tears started to stream down my face. I ran up the steps so I could see the poster in its entirety and focused on the real horse running free! I touched the poster, repeatedly running my fingers along the image of the real horse as my soul desperately attempted to imagine being free.

God will use anything to get our attention and express Himself! He chose a poster to illuminate His plan for me. In speaking His plan, He revealed His character: my Redeemer. This is the main characteristic of God that resonates within me even now. Evil most certainly does exist and it brings about unspeakable events in people's lives. It is hard to understand a loving God in those situations. However, I don't look for the evidence of God in evil, for that comes from Satan and by human hands. Instead, to see evidence of a loving God in those moments, I look at how He turns evil into good in the person's life. That is truly miraculous. That is Divine. That is a Redeemer. I have seen God take the ugliness of my childhood and turn it into beauty. I have experienced Him turning my tears to joy and replacing my spirit of heaviness with a spirit of praise. (Isaiah 61:3). I have experienced Him turning me from a rocking horse – unreal and bound – into a real horse running free! He can do that for you too! He awaits your cry!

I share the previous three illustrations with you to point you towards experiencing Him, to help you discover His character and to encourage you to begin a vibrant personal relationship with the Living God. * He displayed his broken heart for me and ushered in healing before I knew I even needed it. He wooed me to Himself and forever altered our relationship. He revealed His plan for my wholeness. He is the Redeemer of our souls. He pursues us, woos us, and heals us. This is the God that I have come to know.

Throughout the next few years, I filled notebooks with thoughts about God's character. I wrote stories like the ones above, the experiences I have had with Him, and with everything I was learning from His Word. Learning the numerous Names of God, their meanings, and the story of how He revealed a particular name to someone in the Bible was completely life-changing for me. Knowing a particular Name of God is knowing His character. His name reveals the reason He desires healing, the reason He calls us to forgive, the reason

---

See Appendix A for a salvation prayer

for suffering, the reason for trials, the reason for challenges, the reason for gifts, and the reason for blessings. If you know His character, you are better able to understand His purposes for us and His plan for us. All these things can be considered joy when you know the King!

This became my rudder, my source of guidance, in gaining a new perspective on life. This was a biblical perspective.

Rewiring your mind

Another significant area of my healing was replacing my thinking errors with healthy thinking. The Bible refers to this process as the "renewing of your mind" (Romans 12:2). The battle of our minds is vital and on-going. The Bible tells us that Satan is the father of lies. Feeding us lies is his primary focus. Since God's heart and passion is to set us free with the Truth of His Word, then it can be said that Satan's heart and passion is to keep us bound and captive with the power of lies.

As I went through my healing process, I was utterly amazed at how integral the renewing of my mind was. Romans 12:2 says, "Do not conform to the pattern of this world but be transformed by the renewing of your mind." Transformation is directly linked to our minds being renewed. I set out to systematically replace every lie the enemy had fed me during all those years with the Truth of God's Word.

I once again filled notebook after notebook as I wrote down every lie, misconception, and struggle that I was battling with at the time. Then I brought each of those lies before the Lord in prayer, asking Him to show me His Truth from the Bible. This exercise raises awareness of our thoughts and provides us with the opportunity to make the necessary changes to our thought patterns.

I came to learn that thinking patterns are like train tracks in our minds. Each time a specific pattern is repeated, the stronger that track becomes. The stronger the track becomes, the faster the thought races through our mind. In the process, it becomes an automatic thought; no effort is necessary. The only way to change the thought pattern is to literally stop the thought in its track. That is, each and every time the thought left the station and began to race through my mind, I would literally say, "No, stop. I don't want to think like that anymore."

Sometime ago, I was teaching this concept to a nine-year-old boy, a client, who was having a hard time changing some already established habits in his young life. These habits were causing him to get into trouble often, which only made him feel worse about himself. I took out a tablet of paper and began drawing train tracks and a "train of thought" racing over the track. I said to him, "This train is going way too fast and is up to no good. How can I stop this train?"

He looked at the picture and then looked at me, back and forth, and then he jumped from his seat, stood tall and proclaimed, "You say, 'Listen here train, I am the train conductor and I say STOP!'" He smiled and laughed and jumped around a bit. I celebrated with him with much glee! He had gotten it! He returned to the table and began drawing train tracks and a train going much too fast and he yelled "Listen here train, I am the train conductor and I say STOP!" He said this repeatedly for at least ten minutes straight. He was renewing his mind.

Every session after that one, he would begin the session by saying "I am the train conductor, and I told my thoughts to STOP!" This brought him much freedom. It can bring you freedom, too!

One of the most impactful areas in which I renewed my mind was in regard to how I thought of myself. Most people who are abused don't think highly of themselves. They lack confidence and have trouble voicing their opinions or expressing feelings. These negative thought patterns form automatic thinking that speeds much too fast through our minds, "up to no good."

I was curious to discover what God thought of His children. So, I began a new study and filled yet another notebook with verses from the Bible that give us a picture of how He views His children. The verses were both compelling and healing. I began to read them every day and say them out loud to myself over and over again. I would reflect on these verses each time those old ways of thinking tried to persuade me I wasn't worth anything. I would stand in front of a mirror and repeat them. It was hard to comprehend how much God loved me. It was hard to accept His compassion. It was even harder to view myself as:

> *"Chosen by Him"* Ephesians 1:4
> *"Seated with Him in the heavenly places"* Ephesians 2:6
> *"Christ's friend"* John 15:15
> *"Daughter of God"* Romans 8: 14-15
> just to name a few!

I was inspired to compile the most meaningful verses into a document that spoke of how He views His daughter. I inserted my name into the verses and read them often and out loud to fill my mind with these truths.

In numerous women's retreats, I have asked women to insert their names into the verses. Within the safety of trusted relationships, every lady would read them out loud, including her own name. It would often take a long time for each person to get through the list, since tears were usually involved. Deep truths would be revealed as proclamations were made of one's true worth in Christ. It was a life-changing experience for them. I invite you to use this exercise in your life as well.

I call the document, "The Will and Testament of our Lord Jesus Christ." Jesus died on the cross so that these truths would indwell us. He died to give you this inheritance, if you will accept it and receive it. It is yours upon acknowledging the cross and receiving Jesus as your Savior. Once accepted and received, it is important to replace any competing thoughts with the following verses. It is not good enough to simply read it, sign it and never gaze upon it again. It is intended to transform you into His purpose for you: into His image. Won't you accept this invaluable gift?

Gather a few close friends and read the following out loud, one by one, inserting your own name in the appropriate spot. Doing this with friends allows you to gain unconditional support from them as you begin the work of rewiring your mind. This is much like group therapy, and it is a powerful experience to declare who you really are with witnesses surrounding you! I guarantee you won't be the same again.

The Will and Testament of Our Lord Jesus Christ

Through the blood of Jesus Christ "we have obtained an inheritance, having been predestined according to His purpose who works all things after the counsel of His WILL" Ephesians 1:11

This is the inheritance of the Beloved:

1. _____ was chosen in Him before the foundation of the world. Ephesians 1:4
2. _____ is holy and blameless before Him. Ephesians 1:4
3. _____ was predestined for adoption. Ephesians 1:5
4. _____ has redemption through His blood. Ephesians 1:7
5. _____ has forgiveness for_____'s trespasses. Ephesians 1:7
6. _____ is alive together with Christ. Ephesians 2:5
7. _____ was raised up with Him. Ephesians 2:6
8. _____ is seated with Him in the heavenly places. Ephesians 2:6, Philippians 3:20
9. _____ is His workmanship, created in Christ Jesus for good works, which God prepared beforehand, that _____ should walk in them. Ephesians 2:10
10. _____ who was formally far off, has been brought near by the blood of Christ. Ephesians. 2:13
11._____ is a fellow citizen with the saints. Ephesians 2:19
12. _____ is of God's household. Ephesians 2:19
13. _____ has, through Him, access in one Spirit to the Father. Ephesians 2:18
14. _____ has bold and confident access to the Father through faith in Him. Ephesians 3:12
15. _____ is a child of God. John 1:12
16. _____ is Christ's friend. John 15:15
17._____ is the salt of the earth. Matthew 5:13

18. _____ is the light of the world. Matthew 5:14
19. _____ is a part of the true vine, a channel of Christ's life. John 15:1, 5
20. _____ is chosen and appointed by Christ to bear His fruit. John 15:16
21. _____ is a child of God: God is _____ 's Father. Romans 8:14-15, Galatians 3:26, 4:6
22. _____ is a temple – a dwelling place of God–His Spirit and His life dwells in _____ . I Corinthians 6:19
23. _____ is a member of Christ's body. I Corinthians 12:27, Ephesians 5:30
24. _____ is a new creation. 2 Corinthians 5:17
25. _____ is reconciled to God and one in Christ. Galatians 3:26, 28
26. _____ is a child of God and a minister of reconciliation. 2 Corinthians 5:18-19
27. _____ is an heir of God since _____ is a child of God. Galatians 4:6-7
28. _____ is a saint. Ephesians 1:1, I Corinthians 1:2, Philippians 1:1, Colossians 1:2
29. _____ is chosen of God, holy and dearly loved. Colossians 3:12, I Thessalonians 1:4
30. _____ is a child of light and not of darkness. I Thessalonians 5:5
31. _____ is one of God's living stones, being built up in Christ as a spiritual house. I Peter 2:9-10
32. _____ is a member of a chosen race, a royal priesthood, a holy nation, a people of God's own possession. I Peter 2:9-10
33. _____ is an alien and stranger to this world in which _____ temporarily lives. I Peter 2:11
34. _____ is an enemy of the devil. I Peter 5:8
35. _____ is a child of God and _____ will resemble Christ when He returns. I John 3:1-2

36. _____ is born of God, and the evil one--the devil cannot touch _____ . I John 5:18
37. _____ is sealed in Him with the Holy Spirit of promise. Ephesians 1:13
38. _____is not the Great "I AM" (Exodus 3:!4, John 8:24, 28, 58), but by the grace of God, I am what I am. I Corinthians 15:10

On this_____ day of _____ , I hereby accept the inheritance of Jesus Christ upon my life. I choose this day to walk in a manner worthy of the calling with which I have been called. (Ephesians 4:1).

Signed _____

Date _____

How do you feel now that you have read these truths with your own name inserted? Are there some proclamations that stood out to you? Were there some that caused you to choke in disbelief? Were tears rolling down your cheeks? Did you have to pause to absorb the truth of God's Word? Did you stumble over the words?

These are indeed powerful truths! They are not just positive statements. They are living truths bought by the blood of Jesus Christ on the cross for you. He purchased your salvation and your healing. He is not content with saving you and leaving you broken. He desires your healing and wholeness. He desires to see you walk into your purpose. It brings joy to His heart! Embrace these truths. Keep saying them over and over again out loud to yourself or to a trusted friend until you can battle with thoughts that aim to destroy you. I encourage you to battle until these truths begin to define your identity as His child and friend.

As I grew in the confidence to believe these things about myself, I found my voice. I could express my feelings to others, and I began to value myself. That is a remarkable process. It holds tremendous healing.

Discovering the names of God revealed to me the character of God and allowed me to see Him for who He truly is, untainted by my brokenness. Engaging in the arduous work of renewing my mind has had a huge impact on me, but forgiveness was the lynch pin for my healing. It was also the hardest concept to understand and live out. But it was what ushered in and opened the doors to the rest of my healing. I firmly believe that all healing is, in large part, dependent on forgiveness. Therefore, I would like to dedicate the rest of this book to my journey through forgiveness. It is my hope and prayer that in reading these words, healing rooted in forgiveness will come to your life as well.

~ Wrestling through Forgiveness ~

When I first remembered that I had been sexually abused, forgiveness, let me assure you, was not in my thoughts, nor was it my desire. The very thought of forgiving my dad was repulsive and unfathomable. Why should I have to forgive him? If I forgive him, that's letting him off the hook, isn't it? He doesn't deserve to be forgiven. Doesn't forgiveness mean I have to trust him? I don't feel like forgiving him. All those statements were racing through my mind as I tried to reason and justify away what God was calling me to do.

Despite my striving against Him, God continued to pursue me and tried to usher me towards forgiveness for two very long painful and depressing years. One night I had the following dream.

> I was running with the Lord, my hand in His and with my face turned towards Him, looking at Him. I was enjoying the presence of His company immensely. But then for some reason, I turned my face and looked at where we were going – the path of healing paved by forgiveness. I stopped dead in my tracks, looked at Him with anger in my eyes and pulling my hand from His I said, "No, I'm not going down that path."

To say that I was resistant to the idea would be an understatement. Yet, I could sense His pull on my soul.

God's pursuit reached the point of a straightforward confrontation of my heart, mind, spirit, and soul. It happened during a church service. The pastor spoke about the power of the cross. It was certainly not a new concept to me. As he spoke, though, my spirit was stirring. He painted the picture of Jesus' sacrifice to offer us the gift of forgiveness that would prevent us from being separated from Him.

Following the message, we all stood to worship God. As I was worshipping, a heavy conviction of the Holy Spirit overcame me to the point that I fell into my chair. I was deeply convicted of the reality that on one hand, I had freely received forgiveness from God, but on the other hand, I was unwilling to forgive my dad for abusing me. The stark contrast of those two realities pierced my heart and changed my life forever. Jesus died on the cross for my wrongdoing just as much as He died on the cross for my dad's wrongdoing. Who was I then, to receive forgiveness for myself and at the same moment block it from my dad? I realized that while I was refusing to forgive, I wasn't making any progress in my healing; my life was not being rebuilt. As I sat in the chair overcome by this new perspective, I committed to God that I would yield to Him and walk this path of forgiveness. I asked the Holy Spirit to teach me what forgiveness is and what it isn't, since I clearly didn't understand it at all.

Following through with this commitment, I dedicated myself to studying forgiveness from a biblical viewpoint. In that study, I learned that forgiveness in Greek and Hebrew literally means "to send away". The meaning of "to send away" comes from the passage in Leviticus 16:21 that says, *"Then Aaron (a priest) shall lay both of his hands on the head of the live goat and confess over it all the iniquities of the sons of Israel, and all their transgressions in regard to all their sins: and he shall lay them on the head of the goat and send it away into the wilder-*

ness" (NAS). This practice was a significant tradition within Israel for the forgiveness of sin.

It was understood that once the goat left and wandered into the wilderness to die, the sins died as well. The tradition included someone from the area following the goat to ensure it died and then returning to declare that forgiveness was granted to all through the sacrifice of the goat. This of course was only a foreshadow of the sins of the world being placed on the head of Jesus on the cross. He died for the sins of the world and through His death we are forgiven. That is a powerful image of the transformational power of forgiveness. Forgiveness doesn't just happen. It requires sacrifice. It is a sacrifice of all our justifications and reasons why we shouldn't forgive. It is a yielding to the process of forgiveness and all that it holds for us.

I love the definition of "to send away" a lot more than "to let go." To me, "to let go" is passive. Forgiveness is anything but passive. Forgiveness didn't just happen in my life; I was greatly involved in the process.

"To send away" conjures up an image of a box or maybe two, three or even four big boxes! Huge boxes! It conjures up images of packing these boxes with all the hurt, wounds, and emotions of the offense, including any sense of unfairness, betrayal, guilt, abandonment, shame, doubt or insecurity. The boxes are packed with all these offenses. I want you to realize that to place those offenses in the box, you have to face the hurt. You must actively pick it up, name it, acknowledge it, and choose not to allow it to have power over you any longer. If you have ever packed up a room, you know how much effort is involved. Forgiveness is not about ignoring what happened. On the contrary, it demands that you acknowledge the offense and how it has impacted your life.

After the boxes are fully packed, closed, and sealed, then what? Do you address them to the person who hurt you? It seems fair, right? No, God's Word tells us "we don't fight against flesh and blood, but against powers, against the rulers of the darkness of this world, against spiritual wickedness in high places" (Ephesians 6:12).

When writing an address on these boxes, we need to look beyond the person to the one who actually sent it to us. My dad and mom are fully responsible for their actions. It is important, however, to realize that it was Satan himself who authored it against me and sent it to me. The huge boxes need to be addressed to Satan and stamped clearly and profusely with "Return to sender!"

The offense, hurt, and wounds originated with Satan, so "send it away"; send it back to him! Be determined that you no longer want the poison of the offense in your life. Be resolute about no longer wanting to live a life of destruction, illness, brokenness, dead-ends, bitterness, strife, and anger. Set your eyes instead on a life of abundance and fullness. **That** is the box that God sends to you! The hurt and the offense are sent to you by Satan for the purpose of destroying your life. You are not obligated to keep it. Satan sent it to you, so send it back. Say "No thanks, I don't want this in my life anymore!" It will only harm you if you keep holding onto it.

Why Should I Have To Forgive Him?

I asked that question a lot during those two years in which I resisted the process of forgiveness. I tripped over the word "have". "*Why should I have to forgive?*" Can you hear the anger? Can you hear the hurt? Can you hear the indignation? Those feelings are there every time someone asks that question. It's a question that is asked from a place of brokenness. It is a question that is asked while carrying a huge burden that resides in the heart.

The flaw in this question, however, is that it assumes that forgiveness is for the other person. No one wants to do something nice for someone who just hurt them. I didn't want to do anything nice for my dad. He hurt me deeply and nearly destroyed me. Everything within me told me it was just wrong to forgive him. It's not a natural desire to forgive another person. So, again, I ask "Why should I have to forgive him?"

Let's turn the question around. Let's start with the assumption that forgiveness is for the other person. Really? What would that do? What would my forgiveness for my dad do for him? He never acknowledged his wrongdoing, so what would he do with the knowledge that I forgave him? Nothing at all. It would mean absolutely nothing to him, and he would likely discard it, never to think of it again. If forgiveness is for the person who caused the hurt, how would it make sense for the injured party to do all the work of forgiveness just to have the person who caused the hurt simply throw it away without a second thought? That would be cruel and create even more hurt.

Please note that *forgiveness* is for the *one who was hurt*. It's the way out. It is the exit sign flashing before you trying to get your attention. God in His wisdom and mercy created a way for each person to find freedom from the hurt others bring upon us. We have a choice each and every time: do I hold onto the hurt or do I "send it away"?

In John 5:7 we find a paralyzed man who for thirty-eight years followed a singular plan every day of his life. There was pool of water that was known to be occasionally stirred by an angel of God and, at that precise moment, the waters would be imbued with healing powers. His plan was to lower himself into the waters at that exact moment. Every day, for thirty-eight years, he lay in the same spot and played this scene out, waiting for his moment of healing. Despite his sheer determination, he did not receive healing since every time he tried to lower himself into the pool someone else would get in ahead of him. Sadly, the only one who received the healing was the first person into the pool.

Then, after thirty-eight years, a day like any other day began. However, this day would prove to change his life forever. The man was approached by Jesus. Jesus looked at him and asked him a peculiar question: "Do you want to be healed?" **What?** Had he not spent thirty-eight years of his life attempting to do his part towards receiving healing? What else could he possibly do?

He responds to this question by explaining how he has spent the last thirty-eight years of life. He explains he has been at the edge of the pool day in and day out. He explains why his efforts have proven unsuccessful. His answer shows that he is baffled. Jesus doesn't give his response any notice, but simply responds, "Get up, take up your pallet and walk!" Without hesitation, the man does as Jesus says. "Immediately, the man became well and took up his pallet and began to walk!"

I ask you the same question, "Do you want to get well? Seriously, do you?" It may seem like a crazy question to ask.

You may be thinking "I am reading this book, aren't I? I have prayed for the last thirty-eight years for healing. I have been in therapy for the last several years. I have been trying, what else can I do?" You can answer the question. "Do you want to be well?"

You see, everyone will answer "yes" to that question. But not everyone will truly mean it. For those two years that I struggled with God and refused to forgive, I would have screamed "**Yes**, I want to get well." But I really don't think I did. Not to the level that I was willing to do the work that being healed requires. Many other people get stuck here as well. We want an easy fix. We want the pain to go away without having to look at it. The pain threatens us. It is intimidating. But we put up defenses instead and hide it away, hoping it will never surface again.

I remember having a talk with a dear friend about this very thing as I struggled with forgiving. I vividly remember her loving but matter-of-fact words: "Life is easy in the cave hidden away. It is cozy in there. It is familiar. Nothing can hurt you. I get it. It is a risk to come out. It is scary. It is unknown. You might be hurt again. Staying in the cave hurts you too, though. It is dark and lonely. There is no joy in there, no freedom, no light, no health. It's time to come out."

She was completely right. If we are truly honest with ourselves, we would admit that there are benefits to holding onto our hurts and pains. It is somehow satisfying. It feels good. We become comfortable with it. It is familiar. It is easier. People feel bad for us. There are excuses available to us for why our lives aren't working out. We can continue to blame others for our misery and heartbreak. It provides a built-in reason to not connect to others.

We can float through life without any accountability from others, which can be incredibly comfortable. Not having to risk being known by others can be soothing. Holding onto pain and suffering gives us the room to have pity parties for ourselves. Many times, we may even get free passes from others if they know what we have endured. Somehow, we become heroes for enduring the hurt for so long. We are cuddled in life – never pushed to become a better person.

Truly, who would want to give that up? It's a sweet deal.

The paralyzed man had devised a plan, and he followed that plan for thirty-eight years. I wonder how he benefited during those thirty-eight years of life. Let's look at that. He didn't have to work and make a living. He wasn't responsible for anyone but himself. He could just depend on others to meet his needs. He didn't have to be a responsible member of society. His routine was set. It was predictable. It was comfortable.

I had a plan and I followed it for two years. I found it hard to work during those years. I lived with a family to ease the pressure of having to provide for myself. I wasn't pushed to change for quite a long time. I didn't have to face my pain. But neither the plans of the paralyzed man nor my plans worked. Neither one of our plans brought us even a centimeter closer to being healed. We were both just as crippled and broken at the end as on the first day we had started our plan.

Jesus has a plan, too. His plan is to release us from the bondage that hurt and pain places us in. His plan is forgiveness. Later in John 5, the paralyzed man encounters Jesus a second time. Jesus says to him *"You are well, sin no more, so that nothing worse may happen to you."* These words are a recurring theme in the New Testament: "You have been healed; go and sin no more."

Unforgiveness is like a poison. If left inside our body it will cause sickness, injury, and disability. My mom and I both became chronically ill following my abortion. It devastated both of us. I held onto the pain, hurt, abandonment, guilt, and shame; my body literally shut down and manifested these torments with seizures. My mom carried her own sense of guilt and shame, and it impacted her body with cancer. I'm not saying that every time we get sick, we have sinned. I am saying that our bodies and emotions are fundamentally connected. One affects the other. What my mom and I carried was poison and that poison attacked our bodies. Stress, guilt, shame, and unforgiveness have to come out in some way. If they lie dormant, they cause destruction.

"Psychologist Ann O'Leary of Rutgers University is studying the benefits to the immune system of simply talking or writing about physical or mental trauma . . . . The study measures the increase or decrease of disease-fighting white cells in their systems.

Preliminary results show that the women who generally tended to express themselves emotionally about distressing things, and who openly discussed (it)..., had the best immune response to it. Those who tended to be inexpressive and avoided discussing (it) did the worst, said O'Leary, who is working with other researchers in Philadelphia." (Groves, 1996)

The silence in our family was just as toxic as the abuse and trauma. The Bible says, *"When I kept silent my bones wasted away"* (Psalm 32:3). My mental, emotional, spiritual, and physical health steadily returned as I walked deeper into my journey of healing. It all began with breaking the silence, getting it into the open, and wanting to be well.

Our bodies have a better chance of becoming healthy when our emotional and mental well-being is healthy. When I was in Amsterdam with Youth with a Mission, before I remembered the trauma, I attended a prayer meeting led by the top leaders of the base. I requested prayer for healing from the seizures. They enthusiastically prayed for me. As they prayed for me, one of them said, "God will heal you of the seizures. There are some deep dark issues in your family that need to be taken care of first. God has much healing in store for you and the seizures will cease once He has healed you of your wounds."

Wow! Those were amazing words to hear. There was a promise of healing, but a mystery within it. I didn't know what they were talking about! What are the deep dark issues in my family? I was not aware of wounds that need healing! I left disappointed, thinking they were certainly wrong. I was discouraged that the seizures might continue. Little did I know what was in store for my family and me. That message did come true in my life. The seizures ceased once the secrets were revealed. At this writing, I am now thirty-three years seizure free and twenty-three years medication free. That is God's healing in my life that came as a direct result of my walking the path of forgiveness.

"So, why should I have to forgive?" you ask. Well, do you want to be healed? If you do, then embrace the truth that *forgiveness is for yourself, not for the person who hurt you.* If you chose forgiveness. you will discover an abundant life awaits you. God desires to bless you. He waits upon you.

If I Forgive, Aren't I Letting Him Off The Hook?

We often refuse to forgive because we do not want to do anything "good" for the person who hurt us. Relentless protection of our hurt is at the forefront of our mind. I understand. It is almost instinctual. After all, shouldn't the one who hurt us have to face justice, especially if it was a serious offense such as abuse, betrayal, violence, or abandonment?

We choose to stand and hold that person accountable. We let everyone who is willing to listen know what happened and how we were wronged. We cry out for justice. We become obsessed and consumed by the event. We mull it over a thousand times. It bursts into our thoughts, and we feel the hurt all over again. We have to tell someone all about it again and again. Somehow, it never runs out of fuel. Instead, our emotions only intensify over time and soon we become enraged. Justice is no longer what we are seeking; we are now seeking revenge. We start to consider ways of getting even. We start to scheme and plan. Every free moment is dedicated to this cause. It now owns us and drives us.

But who is on the hook? The person who hurt you – or yourself? You are. Hurt has turned to anger and anger has turned to revenge. Revenge now owns you. You are no longer your own. Make no mistake, you are on the hook.

During the first few weeks following the church service in which God heavily convicted me of my unforgiveness, I read Matthew 18:21-35:

> Then Peter came to Jesus and asked, "Lord, how many times shall I forgive my brother or sister who sins against me? Up to seven times?"

> Jesus answered, "I tell you, not seven times, but seventy times seven."

> "Therefore, the kingdom of heaven is like a king who wanted to settle accounts with his servants. As he began the settlement, a man who owed him ten thousand bags of gold was brought to him. Since he wasn't able to pay, the master ordered that he and his

wife and his children and all that he had be sold to repay the debt.

"At this the servant fell on his knees before him. 'Be patient with me,' he begged, 'and I will pay back everything.' The servant's master took pity on him, canceled the debt and let him go.

"But when that servant went out, he found one of his fellow servants who owed him a hundred silver coins.' He grabbed him and began to choke him. 'Pay back what you owe me!' he demanded.

"His fellow servant fell to his knees and begged him, 'Be patient with me, and I will pay it back.'

"But he refused. Instead, he went off and had the man thrown into prison until he could pay the debt. When the other servants saw what had happened, they were outraged and went and told their master everything that had happened.

"Then the master called the servant in. 'You wicked servant,' he said, 'I canceled all that debt of yours because you begged me to. Shouldn't you have had mercy on your fellow servant just as I had on you?' In anger his master handed him over to the jailers to be tortured, until he should pay back all he owed.

"This is how my heavenly Father will treat each of you unless you forgive your brother or sister from your heart." (NIV)

I was stunned by this account. I related to this story in such a poignant way. **I was** the wicked servant – and I hadn't thought seriously about my refusal to forgive my dad. Granted, in human terms, my sins did not compare to what my dad did to me. However, in God's eyes, sin is sin. I had no way of repaying my debt. I was dependent on the cross for my forgiveness. All my attempts to justify myself for not forgiving my dad had ruled my mind for years. I was now face to face with my responsibility to forgive. My unforgiveness had only imprisoned me as if I were in a walled fortress.

I was reminded of a worship time soon after the memories had come back when God impressed upon my mind and heart this picture. It described my life.

> I was standing in the center of a walled city. It was well protected, defended, and very secure. No one could come in, but I couldn't get out either. Suddenly the walls collapsed all around me. I was surrounded by rubble. No longer protected by the massive walls, I was now very vulnerable. I looked around in disbelief and dismay, not knowing what to do or how to rebuild. Knowing no other way, I reached for a brick so that I could stand it upright. As I grasped it, I sensed God saying, "Josee, you have a choice. You can try to rebuild your life on your own or you can walk out from the midst of this rubble and allow me to rebuild your life My way. Will you walk out of the rubble? Will you trust me?" Without fully understanding, I walked out of the rubble, knowing only that I desperately needed God to help me rebuild my life.

As I was reminded of this picture, I realized that I was now truly ready to walk out from the destruction, the pain, the hurt, the betrayal, the abandonment, the guilt, the bitterness, and the loss. I had tried to rebuild my life my way. I had tried to avoid forgiving while seeking healing. I was unsuccessful. I was ready to walk this journey towards forgiveness. I was ready to allow God to rebuild my life His way. I was willing to get out of the prison of my own making. I finally realized that forgiveness is the key that unlocks the prison door.

He Doesn't Deserve Forgiveness!

True enough! However, no one deserves to be forgiven. I don't and you don't. Has anyone in your life, either past or present, extended forgiveness to you for offending them? Did you really deserve that forgiveness? I would venture to say no, you did not. No one does.

We are certainly not deserving of God's forgiveness. His character is of holiness and love. Those two characteristics co-exist together harmoniously in Him. His Holiness demands perfection. He can't even look upon sin. Yet, His love for us is so desperately compelling that He can't live without us. He wants to be with us, and He wants to have us with Him. His love for us drives him to pay the cost that His holiness demands – to satisfy the payment for sin so He can be in relationship with us. That is an amazing, desperate love! He pursues us with an unrelenting love that is rooted in His forgiveness towards us. But we do not deserve one bit of it.

The path of forgiveness is truly a test of our values. Which do we value more: the offense or the relationship? In most instances that is the choice. There are times of course when an ongoing relationship is not possible. That was the case with me and my dad. An ongoing relationship was not possible since he would not acknowledge the abuse and never took responsibility for it. However, I was still faced with the question, "What do I value more, the offense or my healing?"

When we refuse to forgive, we are essentially saying that the offense is so significant I can't move from it; I can't think of anything else; I can't even imagine or think life can possibly be better. We place the offense upon a pedestal and soon our lives are arranged around it. You may not even realize it, but it has happened. Think about it. Do you talk to that person anymore? Have you thrown away their picture and any mementos of them? Do you twitch at the mention of their name and try to change the subject? Do you refuse to sit next to them? You have changed your life patterns due to the offense! You are valuing the offense more than the relationship and, most importantly, more than your healing.

As I have already mentioned, when I moved to Hilo, Hawaii I attended New Hope Christian Fellowship led by Pastor Wayne Cordeiro. He was rather fond of reminding us of how short life is with this illustration.

"Say you took a line, a cable, and shot it out as far in one direction as it could go. Shoot it straight toward the horizon until the end of the cable can no longer be seen. Then take the other end and shoot it in the opposite direction. Now stretch it right through the room you are in and let it pass directly in front of you. It passes through both walls on the opposite ends of the room, stretching into infinity. Now that's what eternity is like! It's forever extending in both directions with no end in sight!

Our life on earth? To contrast the brevity of our earthly dwelling with that of eternity, I would take out my ballpoint pen and draw a vertical scratch on the extended cable. Then I would tell you the width of that vertical scratch (about 1/32nd of an inch) is about how long our life is on this earth in comparison with eternity. That's right. Not very long!

But do you know what most people do? They not only live on scratch, but they love that scratch. They kiss the scratch. They save for that scratch. They hoard for that scratch. They live scratch lives, have scratch businesses, and have scratch families with scratch hopes and scratch dreams. "(Cordeiro, 1998)

Now, I have a question. Is the offense you are holding onto, simply because the person who hurt you doesn't deserve to be forgiven, worth the tiny width of a scratch from a pen on the cable of life? That gives perspective, doesn't it? No one deserves forgiveness. But it is a powerful gift that brings abundant life to the one who chooses to forgive!

Pastor Wayne Cordeiro is an amazing pastor. He is filled with tremendous love and compassion. He has a passion for those who have yet to make a profession of faith and he has a heart for the broken. I was broken when I came to his church. I was in a million pieces. I had difficulty with any type of relationship, but even more so with males and those in a position of authority. Pastor Wayne was both male and in a position of authority. He had no chance! I did everything I could think of to push him away. I was rude to him, I judged him in my heart, and I walked away from him when he was approaching me on various occasions. But he never altered his view of me. He loved me no matter what.

A few years later, in Honolulu, Hawaii (he had moved there to start a sister church and I had moved there a few years after that), I felt that I had to take care of this. I needed to take responsibility for how I had mistreated him. I was now in a different place in my healing. I wrote him a letter expressing my sorrow. He responded in a letter that I still have today. Here is an excerpt.

> *"Thank You for your deepest and most sincere apologies. I accept them fully and in the same breath want to let you know that I took no offense at all. God is so faithful to help us love others through their hurts. It's His grace and great love that power me on. Yet I so want to honor your heartfelt apologies, so I do accept them. Please be free of any guilt or feelings of condemnation knowing that they are not from God, nor from me. You have lovingly resolved those issues; now move forward with all boldness in Christ!"*

Wow! I read that letter over and over again, each time with tears streaming down my face as I was released from my self-imposed prison. Did I deserve his forgiveness? Not at all! But Pastor Wayne modeled to me that he valued our friendship more than the offense. He modeled to me God's complete grace and love towards us. I am deeply thankful for that and for him!

I want you to notice something though. In his choice to forgive me as soon as the offenses took place, it allowed him to remain free. When my letter reached his desk years following the offense, it wasn't a heart wrenching struggle for him to write those freeing words to me. He had already chosen forgiveness the moment the offense had taken place. He didn't harbor any bitterness or unforgiveness, nor did he hold any against me.

Do you know how I know that? Because with resolute determination he extended love, grace, and compassion to me no matter how I treated him. He never wavered in it. I benefited from his choice to forgive. In extending forgiveness towards me, he extended freedom to me: freedom from guilt and self-condemnation. Do you see the picture? Do you get the power? Don't you want to be free?

Colossians 3: 12-14 points us towards how we are to interact with one another. It encourages us to show *"compassion, kindness, humility, gentleness and patience. Bear with each other and forgive one another if any of you has a grievance against someone. Forgive as the Lord forgave you. And over all these virtues put on love, which binds them all together in perfect unity"* (NIV).

How can we show compassion if we harbor an offense? How can we show kindness if we harbor a hurt? How can we be humble if we can't extend forgiveness to one another? How can we be gentle if we are angry? How can we be patient if we are fuming in frustration? We can't!

Do you see how unforgiveness damages relationships? Do you see how unforgiveness only creates more injury towards yourself? Pastor Wayne was able to show me compassion, kindness, humility, gentleness, patience, love, and forgiveness long before I even asked for his forgiveness. In doing so, he was free from the offense.

Doesn't Forgiveness Mean I Have To Trust That Person Again?

It is often assumed that forgiveness and trust are inextricably linked. However, that is highly misleading. Forgiveness is a choice to no longer hold onto the offense. It is a choice to be free from the impact of the offense. Trust, on the other hand, means having "assured reliance on the character." Trust is earned and should be based on the character of a person. It should be based on how a person treats another person. Do they honor your privacy? Do they respect you? Are they honest? Do they take responsibility for their actions? Do they ask for forgiveness? Do they have your best interest at heart? Do they care about your needs? Are they there for you when you need them? Are they available to you?

If the answer to those questions is yes, then they are generally trustworthy. If the answer is no, you can still choose to forgive that person without making yourself vulnerable to them. To trust a person who hasn't shown himself to be trustworthy isn't wise. To place yourself at risk of being mistreated, harmed, demeaned, or taken advantage of isn't required of anyone. To do so is actually to devalue yourself, which has its own ramifications.

I forgave my dad. But by forgiving him, I didn't build a relationship with him. If he had taken responsibility for his actions, expressed remorse, or asked for forgiveness, a relationship could carefully have been considered with intentional boundaries. You see, I didn't have to build a relationship with him as proof of my forgiveness.

I encourage you to sever thinking patterns that link forgiveness and trust together. They are not the same thing; trust does not always follow forgiveness. It can be dangerous to place trust in an untrustworthy person. You must use common sense and not allow religious duty or allegiance to dictate whom you trust.

Joseph in the Old Testament is a perfect example of this. He was sold into slavery by his own brothers. This event led to a series of terrible experiences for him. But he met each one of them with forgiveness. We will look at that more closely later. What I want to focus on now is how he separated forgiveness and trust. His forgiveness towards his brothers was evident, as years later during a famine in a nearby country his brothers came to Egypt in search of food.

Joseph at that time was second in command only to Pharaoh. As his brothers approached Joseph, they didn't even recognize him, thinking he was long dead. However, Joseph recognized them. He put into place a series of pointed tests to discern their character.

He tested their honesty, their regard for each other, their humility, and their ability to take responsibility for their actions. He tested their loyalty to one another and their willingness to protect the youngest of them, who was his only full brother. Only after they demonstrated growth in character and the characteristics of trustworthiness did he reveal himself to them. His brothers were deeply afraid of him as he could have killed all of them right then with absolutely no repercussions.

He demonstrated his forgiveness by ushering them to a banqueting table full of the best food. Remember, this was during a time of profound famine. Food was scarce. He also sent them home with an abundance of provisions to meet their needs and more. Joseph knew that forgiveness and trust are worlds apart. *Forgiveness is proven within your own heart, whereas trust is proven within the character of the other person.*

I Don't Feel Like Forgiving!

Hey, I hear you! I really, really do! However, I have some news for you: forgiveness is not an emotion. It doesn't just wash over you in an extraordinary moment of life. No one wakes up one day and says "Okay, today I feel like forgiving". *Forgiveness is a conscious choice, a choice that requires a great deal of determination.*

As I walked the path of forgiveness, I learned that forgiveness can't be based on feelings. I couldn't wait for the desire to forgive to just happen to overcome me one morning. It would never happen. I would still be waiting. Rather, I learned that *forgiveness is an absolute choice.* It is rarely accompanied by good feelings or even satisfaction. It is a battle to the end. I had to willfully choose to forgive my dad with great determination and even pain. The choice was often accompanied by streaming tears or a deep sigh of surrender. It wasn't an easy choice, but one that had to be made – every day – for a while – and often several times in the same day. *In the face of hurt, in the face of anger, my choice had to be forgiveness, so that I could be free.* Walking this path of forgiveness for the next several years became the most important thing I have done in my life. Nothing else that I have accomplished in my life compares to the freedom I received through the work of forgiveness. It held the key to my healing. It was a fight for my soul!

I want to remind you of or introduce you to a children's book *The Little Engine that Could* by Watty Piper. The story is about a train engine, carrying toys to children, which breaks down going over the mountain. The toys are desperate to get to the children and they stop every engine along the tracks and ask if it will pull the train. One engine after another turns them down, despite their ability to accomplish the task. At last, a little blue engine comes along. The toys doubt his ability but ask him anyway. He says he has never left the engine yard before. He says his job is simply to move train cars from one track to another. Despite his inexperience, he decides to give it a try. He faces many challenges along the way and develops the mantra, "I think I can, I think I can" to help him push through and get over the peak of the mountain. Of course, the little blue engine is successful!

I want you to notice a few things in this story. The first thing is that the little engine says that he has never left the train yard. Unforgiveness can be the same. How many times have you reasoned away why you don't have to forgive? What is the result? You stay in the train yard; you can't get out. You develop a thinking pattern much like that in a train yard. One train of thought leads you to another and another and eventually you are right back to the first train of thought. The loop of tracks limits you. You are stuck. You can't leave. You will spend your life traveling the same tracks over and over again.

As long as the engine stayed in the train yard, he missed his purpose in life. He had no idea that he held the potential to climb that mountain. If he had said no to this opportunity he would have missed out on the plan for his life. The same is true with unforgiveness. It holds us back from realizing our purpose and potential. The plan for our life becomes severely limited. Once the engine was presented with another possibility, however, he seized upon it, worked on it, set his determination and followed through to the end. In that act, he not only changed his own life, but made it possible for the toys to fulfill their purpose in making the children happy.

And so it is, each time a person chooses to forgive. In choosing the path of forgiveness, you are set on a path that is challenging and perhaps seemingly impossible. Forgiveness can seem like that steep mountain that challenged the little blue engine so severely. It requires determination, work, and follow-through to realize the blessings on the other side. It holds promise but requires a choice of your will. In choosing forgiveness, you not only change the direction of your life, but you also have the potential to change the lives of those around you.

Again, I want you to ponder that the little blue engine had never been out of the train yard. He had never seen what lay on the other side of the mountain. He had to travel the tracks to experience what life held for him. You will never realize your full potential in life until you travel the path of forgiveness. I guarantee that if you make a commitment to travel this path, your life will be blessed. You will discover new places, new blessings, and new beginnings. It is time to get out of the train yard of unforgiveness and experience what the land of forgiveness holds for you.

Also notice that the engine pulled other train cars with it. That is my hope. I hope to bring others out of their train yards of unforgiveness with this book. I hope to encourage you to start your engine. It is time! Get out! I encourage you to bring others with you out of their train yards of unforgiveness as well.

In contrast to the little engine's mantra "I think I can, I think I can," Philippians 4:13 says, "In Christ I can do all things." We are commanded to forgive, not as a rule but as an invitation. In the most pressing words imaginable we are invited to forgive by God Himself so that we can be free! We aren't just urged and left to figure it out on our own. No, we are urged, invited and commanded and then given the power to accomplish it. Jesus Christ walks with us along this path of forgiveness. Remember my dream? Who was with me? Jesus!

Who was holding my hand? Jesus! I wasn't alone and neither are you. He is with us, and He will never leave us. Lean on Him and He will strengthen you!

~ The Gift of Forgiveness Unwrapped ~

Forgiveness Is A Command Wrapped Up As A Gift.

Healing cannot take place completely without forgiveness. When we haven't forgiven, we have not "sent away" the hurt yet. Instead, we harbor it in our hearts, holding onto it, protecting it, defending it, justifying it. The hurt keeps hurting. The doors to our heart are closed, which prevents the hand of God from healing the hurts. Abundant life eludes us. With forgiveness we choose to "send away" the hurt. In doing so, we open up our heart and create an avenue through which Jehovah Rapha, our Healer, can come and touch our hurt and heal it.

In the dream I had, Jesus wasn't just sending me off by myself to face this journey alone. He was right there beside me, holding my hand, willing to be my constant companion. He is fully prepared to help us every step of the way. I refused Him because I failed to realize that *forgiveness is a command wrapped up as a gift.* It is a gift that comes from the heart of a loving God who desires the best for each of us. His voice isn't harsh and demanding. No, His is a voice that calls to us as loving parents would call to a child to prevent him or her from pain. If you listen carefully, you will see that there is a loving protectiveness in His command of forgiveness.

Joseph in the Old Testament understood that. Joseph was a man who suffered many wrongs yet met each one with forgiveness. Joseph suffered three main offenses. The first one was at the hands of his brothers, who sold him into slavery out of deep-seated jealousy. Joseph responded by allowing God to walk him through the hurt and pain to forgiveness. As a result, Joseph was free to turn the offense into a blessing. Due to his integrity of character, he was soon promoted to supervisor over all of Pharaoh's servants (Genesis 39:4).

The second offense was at the hand of the wife of a high-ranking officer of Pharaoh, who falsely accused Joseph of making sexual advances towards her. As a result, he was thrown into prison. Again, Joseph walked with God through the hurt and pain and was able to forgive. As a result, Joseph was free to turn the offense into a blessing. Due to his integrity, he was soon promoted once again as supervisor over all of the prisoners (Genesis 39: 21-22).

The third offense came at the hand of a cupbearer who had promised to mention Joseph to Pharaoh. The cupbearer broke that promise, which resulted in a longer prison term. Joseph was faithful to forgive and was for a third time free to turn the offense into a blessing. For a third time, his character was noticed and he was promoted to second in command to Pharaoh over all of Egypt (Genesis 41: 39-40).

At this time, Egypt and the surrounding nations were facing a serious life-threatening drought. While Egypt had plenty, all the surrounding nations were suffering. How is it that Egypt was overflowing with provision? It was because Joseph was attuned to God's voice. Joseph had been diligent in listening to God to store up the surplus of crops for years prior to the drought. As a result, Egypt had such an abundance of food during the drought that they were not only able to provide for themselves, but also for the nations around them.

Joseph's brothers, however, were living in a neighboring nation and experiencing severe drought. Driven by need, the brothers made the trek to Egypt. They had no idea who they would encounter there. Joseph recognized his brothers immediately. However, they didn't recognize him. Joseph had the advantage of the element of surprise as well as a position of power and authority. He carefully chose his next move.

Surprisingly, he didn't exact harm on them. Nor did he seek revenge, although he easily could have. No. Instead, he chose to face his brothers in peace and save them from starvation by providing their essential needs. He would not have been able to do that if he hadn't already forgiven.

We witness a profound moment when Joseph revealed his identity. His brothers were expecting revenge. They were certain he would kill them or imprison them. He did no such thing. Instead, he chose forgiveness. He said, *"And as for you, you meant evil against me, but God meant it for good in order to bring about this present result, to preserve many people alive"* (Genesis 50:20). Joseph thereby became a blessing to his family, to his nation, and to the nations around him because of forgiving those who had hurt him and having received healing from those wounds. That is immensely profound.

It says four times in God's Word, *"...and the Lord was with Joseph."* Joseph allowed God to be his constant companion in every offense. Joseph forgave, and God gave him success within each offense. God didn't take him out of the offensive situations, but instead caused Joseph to be a blessing within them. Joseph knew that *forgiveness is a command wrapped up like a gift.*

As I began to walk my path of forgiveness, Joseph became my role model. I prayed often that God would help me make the choice that Joseph made every day. Each time I felt the poisonous sting of unforgiveness creep into my heart I would stop and say out loud, "I choose to forgive my dad for...," filling in the blank with the particular hurt that was in my mind and heart.

The hurt and wounds of abuse are so numerous that it is impossible to forgive the whole offense in one fell swoop. Each part of the offense needs to be forgiven. Many hurts are that way. A simple harsh word can cause a myriad of hurt in a person. What needs to be forgiven isn't just the harsh word that was spoken, but its impact. Emotions such as guilt, shame, embarrassment, being belittled, and many others, need to be dealt with individually and specifically. Words hold within them the power to either inspire or destroy.

As I forgave each day, and often many times each day, it wasn't because I was releasing the hurt and offense, taking it back, releasing it again, and so on. Each time I forgave my dad, I was forgiving another facet of the hurt. Abuse is a devastating wound and the depths to which it cuts are nearly unfathomable. So, my forgiveness had to plunge the depth of the wounds. That required a process, not just a moment when I was suddenly free of the hurt. And it was because it was a process that forgiveness seemed so unappealing. We want instant release from pain. But forgiveness requires commitment. With the same determination as Joseph, I kept my eyes on my freedom and chose the path of forgiveness. As I walked this path, I discovered many gems along the way.

Forgiveness Is A Safeguard For Your Soul.

Psalms 23:4 says, *"Your rod and your staff, they comfort me"* (NAS). Have you ever wondered how or why? A staff is just a stick, for crying out loud!! How can a stick comfort me?

That is what ran through my mind as I was reading my Bible one day. I asked God how it is possible. I heard Him say, "Look at who is holding the stick." So, I broadened the picture to see the shepherd holding it. Then I broadened the picture again to see where he was leading the sheep: to green pastures and still waters.

As I pondered this, I understood that unforgiveness, hurts, wounds, a broken relationship, unfulfilled expectations – all those and more – can lead us off the side of a cliff into a thorn bush or into a desert. None of these are typically desired destinations. The shepherd, however, leads the sheep into green pastures and still waters. How? With his staff!

When the sheep feel the staff along their side directing them, they know they are being protected. God is the Good Shepherd and throughout our lives we also will feel that "stick," that staff, prodding us in a certain direction. That brings comfort because we know He would never lead us into danger or harm. Instead, He leads us into a place of rest, peace, healing, joy, fulfillment, and purpose. I would encourage you to allow Him to lead you down the path of forgiveness. Remember to pick up the many gems along the way, for there are many.

One of my favorite stories in the Bible isn't a typical favorite. It is the story of Cain and Abel. There is an amazing gem hidden within this story. We usually think of the two brothers as the only characters. If that were true, there wouldn't be much within it to constitute it being a favorite story. When you realize there is a third character in this story and who He is, well, that profoundly changes its entire meaning. The third character is God himself. What is revealed about God in this story is deeply beautiful and transformational. What really stands out to me in this story is that God actively pursues Cain, trying to lead him on a different path.

In Genesis 4:5, Cain is rather angry at his brother and God. In verse 6, God acknowledges Cain's anger and warns him of what is ahead if he continues on this path. He encourages him to turn away from his anger and towards forgiveness. Cain doesn't listen. He doesn't heed the Shepherd's staff but continues on his own path and kills his brother. Yet God, filled with both sadness and love for Cain, is not willing to leave him alone. God continues to pursue Cain and prompts him to confess his sin (verse 9). Cain again refuses the staff. In verse 10, God gives him the opportunity to once again confess and receive forgiveness. Cain still refuses. So, in verses 11-12, after pursuing Cain three times and getting the same response all three times, only then does God banish Cain from the region. This was not for killing his brother, however, but because of unrepentance.

Did you catch that? Unrepentance drove him out, not his original sin. God was prepared to forgive Cain had he repented. It is probable that Cain wouldn't even have had to leave the area. In verse 13, Cain, in desperation, cries out for mercy—but not in repentance. God, in His unfathomable and gracious love for Cain, grants him protection from his fears. Even though there is no indication that Cain has repented, God still shows him mercy. That is true love!

The story of Cain and Abel exemplifies God's heart toward us. He cries out to us to forgive for He knows that forgiveness safeguards us against walking a path of self-destruction. He pursues us. He uses His rod and staff to direct us away from the path of anger and destruction and towards the path of forgiveness. God pursued Cain both before and after his act of violence. God's heart was towards Cain and God's heart is toward us.

"Your rod and your staff, they comfort me." Indeed!

Forgiveness Is A Path To Your Own Healing.

The analogy of the potter and the clay gives an amazing picture of the relationship between God and his children. As a potter holds clay in his hands, he holds a grand vision for the drab piece of clay. With great patience and gentleness, he shapes it until that vision becomes a reality. Everything in our lives shapes us, either for good or for harm.

The sexual abuse I experienced marred me in countless ways and shaped me into a broken vessel. It negatively affected my thinking, my perceptions, my attitudes, my beliefs, my decisions, and my relationships. My unforgiveness further shaped me into a fractured vessel, for it made room for bitterness, wrath, guilt, and a hardness of heart towards God and others. This resulted in self-imposed isolation and loneliness.

Jeremiah 18:4 says, *"But the pot he was shaping from the clay was marred in his hands; so the potter formed it into another pot, shaping it as seemed best to him"* (NIV). God wasn't content to leave me as a broken vessel when He knew the beauty He intended and the potential He placed within me. As painful as it was to allow God to push and knead areas of my life that needed to be refashioned, it was worth it. This process brought amazing healing in my life. *Forgiveness is the path through which God can redeem your hurts and reshape them into beauty.*

Our lives are so intertwined with each other. We constantly influence one another in everything that we do. If we remain in hurt and bitterness, we impact those around us negatively. My dad chose that course in his life. As a result, my siblings, my mom and I paid a very high price. But if we choose courage and allow God to bring healing to our lives, we will be able to impact others with hope, life, and truth. Oh my, how my family would have been different if my dad had chosen that path!

It was always my heart's desire for God to take my hurt and pain and somehow turn them into good. God has done just that. Since walking my path of healing, I have had the opportunity to encourage other women who have been abused and usher them through the rebuilding process. The women also had much to forgive. As they made that choice, healing came into their lives as well.

I have also had the amazing experience of sharing my story publicly in various venues. Each time I share my story, waves of people come to me and share their hurts, pain, and wounds. It has been an honor for me to point them towards forgiveness and ultimately healing. After an initial conversation with each person, many return again and again, keeping me posted on their journey towards forgiveness. I am always blessed by this show of trust. It brings tears to my eyes as I hear story after story of forgiveness, repaired relationships, hope, and healing. These in turn told others of the transformational power of forgiveness they experienced firsthand.

The opportunity to speak into other people's lives is humbling and profound. It would never have happened had I not embraced the gift of forgiveness. It has been a tremendous blessing to see God take my hurt and pain and use them as an ointment on another person's life. Only God can do that!

My experiences inspired me to pursue a career in therapy. As a Licensed Marriage and Family Therapist, I have been able to have a part in reshaping people's lives in a way that reflects God's beauty and purpose. This has been incredibly fulfilling for me.

Writing this book has also flowed directly from my desire to see others healed by God's hand. Everything within our lives is meant to impact those around us – to encourage, inspire, comfort, breath faith, bring healing, and nourish. Our lives are a parable; each one of us has a message to share with the world. My message is that God desires to bring healing in people's lives. My message became my passion. It fills me with indescribable joy to share what God has done in my life – to share my experiences with others so that they too will be inspired to believe God to do the same in their lives.

What is your purpose? What is your message? What is your parable? What is God wanting to shape and mold in you so that your purpose, message, and parable can be clearly seen and understood? What work do you need to do so that you can be free to walk in the path He holds for you? He is your potter; you are the clay. Are you yielding your life to Him? Are you allowing His work to be fulfilled in you? Are you His vessel?

Forgiveness is the path through which God can redeem your hurts and reshape them into beauty. Are you ready to see a miracle of beauty come from your hurt? Allow Him to do His work in you.

Forgiveness Is Choosing Not To Act On The Offense.

Many people struggle with another thinking pattern related to forgiveness: that forgiveness is synonymous with forgetting. In fact, many people are resolute in their stance of unforgiveness because they know they can't forget what happened. My book itself is proof that I haven't forgotten my hurts and wounds – but I have forgiven. Forgiving and forgetting is not the same thing.

The mind itself is not physically capable of forgetting information except, perhaps, as a result of trauma or illness. Your mind has stored every single experience throughout your life. Some memories are stronger than others. Some can be recalled in a moment's notice, whereas others require reminders from some outside source. Most memories can be brought back to the forefront of your mind with the right stimulus. So why are some memories strong and others weak? That completely depends on what we choose to focus on.

Remember what we discussed about thinking patterns? Those patterns are formed by repetition. If we focus on a memory day to day, week to week, and month to month and from one year to the next, that memory will remain strong in our mind and our emotions will continue to be stimulated by that memory. If we choose to not recall a memory it may recede from our mind, but it is never completely erased. So, it is unrealistic to think that the choice of forgiving will cause you to forget the offense. It just doesn't happen that way.

God's Word is filled with verses that say God forgets our sins, such as Hebrews 8:12 which says, "*I will remember their sins no more*" (NAS). In contrast, Jeremiah 14:10 says, "*Now the Lord will remember their sins and call their sins to account"* (NAS). This is an important point.

What determines when God remembers and when He doesn't? What does the statement "God forgets" mean? If we don't forget, how does God forget? In the above referenced passage of Jeremiah, God had been pursuing the people of Israel and lovingly calling them to cease sinning and turn back to Him. The people of Israel refused His cries to them again and again. God sent the prophet Jeremiah to persuade them, but still they refused to change their ways. In their choice, consequences followed. Yet, even though they chose to ignore God's instruction, He still extended His mercy to them. Healthy discipline from a parent is intended to teach a child about their wrong choice so that the child's life improves. Discipline isn't the same thing as punishment. Punishment has at its core vengefulness. Discipline has the heart of a teacher. So, it is with the heart of God towards His people when He "remembers" our sins.

The passage we spoke of in Hebrews, on the other hand, tells of God's response to those who do admit their wrong-doing and change their behavior, heart, and attitude. In that verse, God chooses to not remember their sins anymore. He is like the loving parent who sees in his child an acknowledgement of wrongdoing, remorse, and a desire to learn how to do it differently. In this situation, there is little to no need for consequences. Instead, it is a teachable moment within a loving embrace.

God's mercy is seen in both situations. When He remembers, he does so to lovingly discipline His people for their own well-being. When He chooses to not remember it is in response to a heart that has already acknowledged wrongdoing and is seeking how to correct it.

Now that we have a context, let's look at this word "remember." In comparing the differences between these two verses it becomes clear that the term "remember" is not used literally here. God's brain synapses don't suddenly fail to work, erasing the memory of our sin. It isn't that God becomes ignorant of our wrongdoing and can no longer recall it. If that were true, then Jesus would not have needed to die on the cross for our sins at all. We could just wait for God's brain to go on the fritz and forget all our wrongdoings!

So, if "remembering" is not a literal translation, what does it refer to?

When God says that He *"will remember their sin no more,"* God extends forgiveness. God doesn't act against the person who has sinned. No discipline comes their way. "Remembering their sin no more" implies that God will not discipline, will not hold that sin against us, and will not act on it. That isn't the same as forgetting. God doesn't forget our sins. That is good news since if it was just forgetting, He could just as suddenly remember one day and exact punishment towards us unexpectedly. But He remembers our sin and then makes a loving and merciful choice to not act on our sin. Due to the death and resurrection of Jesus Christ, and our belief that leads us to receive His forgiveness, our relationship with God is not altered due to our sin. He forgives and calls us back to Himself with great compassion.

There is another verse that depicts a beautiful picture of how God responds once He has forgiven. Psalms 103:12 says, "As far as the east is from the west, so far has He removed our transgressions from us" (NAS). It is important to note that the east and west can never meet since they go on forever. Once God forgives our sin, He chooses to never act on it: not ever! He doesn't hold it against us; He doesn't save it for the next time we mess up to just remind us again. He forgives. In His forgiveness, it is as if it never happened. He chooses to relate to us as if we never sinned.

One day while visiting the San Diego Zoo, I witnessed complete chaos inside the elephant enclosure. Two of the three elephants were fighting with each other. The enclosure had two levels. One of the elephants was on the lower level reaching up to the elephant above it and attempting to force it out of balance as it pushed one of its front feet with its head. The elephant above would kick it and roar with an unforgettable angry tone.

This went on for several minutes until the third elephant came running (if you can imagine this) and clearly scolded both of them. He seemed to act as referee between the two as they sorted out their disagreement. Suddenly the loudness of their "discussion" ceased. There was a quiet moment, then all three of them bounded around the exhibit with much energy and a distinct lightness to their play.

I doubt the two elephants "forgot" the offense as they played together. They simply choose to not act on the offense towards each other. They chose the relationship as more important than the offense and they had a great time together! *Forgiveness is not forgetting the offense but choosing not to act on the offense.*

This does not mean that we continue a relationship with the person who hurt us *if it isn't safe to do so.* What it does mean is that we choose to not hold onto the offense within ourselves. It means that we no longer dwell on the offense. It means that we allow the memories to recede into our mind instead of being at the forefront of our thoughts, negatively impacting our attitudes, behaviors, relationships, and health. It means that we no longer proceed through life from the perspective of being a wounded soul, but rather, we live our lives free from the hurt.

Forgiveness Restores Life To Your Soul.

As I sat with my friends during the lunch period of my freshmen year of high school, I became acutely aware of how different I was from them. They talked freely with each other, laughing, open, trusting, and secure. I marveled at their abilities to be so nonchalant with one another. I, on the other hand, was so self-conscious and guarded that it was difficult to even create a flow in any conversation. Everything I shared had to be censored for fear of exposing what was happening in my home. I was deeply saddened at the stark difference between my friends and me, and at a complete loss as to how to become more like them.

As lunch ended, I walked into my science class, sat in the back row and wrote this poem.

Looking Out the Window

I look out the window
I see the snow flurries coming down.
I see the happy faces of the children
I long to join them, run with them, laugh with them.
I long to feel the white, wet snow against my boot.
I long to form a single snowball within my hands.

I long to make a snowman, to go sleighing.

But I can not join the children in the snow.
Because I cannot walk.
I am paralyzed.
But that is okay, because I can do things they cannot.
And perhaps I will learn to walk
and join the happy faces in the snow.

This poem captures my brokenness. I remember showing it to my immediate and extended family members. Everyone liked it. I thanked them, but inside I was screaming, *"Don't you get what I am saying?", "Can't you hear me?", "Won't you help me?"* I couldn't explain it to anyone at the time, of course, since I was simply trying to survive each day. I even submitted the poem to the school paper, but they rejected it, stating that it was too sad to print. I was crying out for help in the only way I knew how. But no help came.

I kept this poem close to me throughout the years. *Paralyzed* is the best word I can think of to describe what abuse does to a person. It imprisons you. It prevents you from making friends, keeping friends, and doing well in life. It creates an overall sense of worthlessness. It paralyzes you in every area of life. I could barely function like a normal person – let alone be able to excel in any area of life. The last line in the poem: "But that is okay, because I can do things THEY cannot," was a self-protective statement. It was a lie I told myself so that I wouldn't feel completely worthless. The only problem was that I had no idea what I was good at.

When I was in therapy shortly after breaking the silence of the abuse, my counselor painted a verbal picture that described my life. She said I was "lying in a coffin waiting to die." That was a scary statement, and it rattled me to my core. She was right. It is a great picture of what brokenness feels like. It isn't exactly death. But it is preparing for it, taking on the attitude of death, and being resigned to it.

In the Old Testament, Pharaoh was a term used to refer to the ruler over Egypt, much like we use the term President today. In Egypt, the Israelites were the slaves of Pharaoh. He held them prisoner to his every whim for decades. The Israelite slaves built Egypt, in all of its grandeur, yet benefitted little from it. But God raised Moses to be His spokesman. And through Moses, God entreated Pharaoh to set the Israelites free.

A battle ensued between Pharaoh and Moses, with the wellbeing of the Israelites hanging in the balance. So, to get Pharaoh's attention, God struck the land of Egypt with ten devastating plagues, each intended to cause Pharaoh to release the Israelites from slavery. Each time, Pharaoh would relent, saying he would let the Israelites go, then change his mind and refuse to let them go. God would respond by releasing yet another plague. Pharaoh would relent, and then once again change his mind when the plague ended. This went on for ten plagues.

The plague of locusts devoured all the livestock and produce throughout the country. This caused starvation and death across the land. In desperation, Pharaoh called Moses before him and said, "I have sinned against the Lord your God and against you, now therefore, please forgive my sins only this once, and make supplication to the Lord your God, that He would only remove this death from me" (Exodus 10:16-18, NAS).

Pharaoh was referring to the death of the livestock and agriculture. However, I think Pharaoh stumbled upon a profound truth. He knew that it was due to his disobedience to God that these plagues were being released upon his land and his people. He was aware of what was required of him to bring an end to the plague. He would have to repent – and in repenting, life would return.

The same is true of forgiveness. *Forgiveness restores life.* Forgiveness washes away the effects of hurt and wounds. Forgiveness is the breath of hope for restoring physical health and it holds the possibility of restoring relationships. Forgiveness is the key that unlocks the prison door. Forgiveness restores your purpose in life. Forgiveness restores your relationship with God. Forgiveness is a life-giving breath from the Giver of life itself.

Through forgiveness, healing was made possible for me. In that healing, I no longer feel different from others. I no longer feel paralyzed. I can join my friends in laughter, joy, peace, and comfort, knowing that I am free to be myself. I am no longer held back by my wounds and hurts.

Forgiveness is the ultimate gift. It is a profound one. It is for you. If you only accept one gift in your life, be certain it is this one. There is truly no other gift that even compares. Forgiveness is what Jesus Christ offers each and every person in order to ensure the possibility of a relationship with us. Jesus Christ died on the cross to forgive us of our sins. In forgiveness, you enter into an interactive relationship with the Living God who created you, loves you and desperately wants to know you. He desires to heal your hurts and release you into your purpose. Living for that purpose will fulfill you and bring you great joy! Forgiveness is life itself.

In the remaining pages, you will find the miracles that God brought into my life through my choice of forgiveness. You will find God's faithfulness to me as I allowed Him to rebuild my life in His way. You will discover the freedom I received from the hurts and pain of the past. And you will experience how God kept His promise to "cause all things to work together for good to those who love God, to those who are called according to His purpose" (Romans 8: 28, NAS).

SECTION THREE
Daybreak

The Soul's Fight

Dad

I sat before the house with awe and wonderment.

The house that held us captive
    When we desired for escape.
The house that held the secrets
    That bound us in our shame.
The house that tore us apart
    When it should have made us strong.
The house that demanded payment
    When it should have offered love.

I sat before the house with sadness in my heart for I realized
    The house in which he ruled,
        Now rules him.
    The house in which he betrayed us,
        Now betrays him.
    The house in which he tore us apart,
        Now tears him apart.
    The house in which he demanded payment,
        Now demands payment from him.

I sat before the house with questions in my heart
Questions I never dared to ask …
    I ask you, Dad . . .
        What was the reason?
        What were you thinking?
        What was the thrill?
        Where were your morals?
        Where were your ethics?
        How could you do this to your little girls?

I sat before the house. . . No longer in the house
    We have escaped.
    We hold no more shame.
    We have pulled together.
    WE HAVE BEEN OFFERED LOVE!
We stand outside that house - free and set apart.

But he, Dad, remains inside –
Reaping what he sowed.

The Soul's Fight

~ Freedom ~

I wrote that poem just seven months after the memories of my past had surfaced. I was sitting in my car on the street, facing our house. My dad didn't know that I was there. I wasn't there to visit him. I was there to give voice to my soul. I was there to see the house without the veil of secrecy over it. My heart and soul were hurting and I was trying to find my way back. As I sat there, the words flowed onto the paper and I again became aware of the damage he had caused my siblings and me.

I am proud of my siblings and myself for having found the courage to take a stand and care about our own souls. I am sure my dad didn't see this coming. I am sure he was caught off guard. It was the right time, though. It was time to heal.

Six years after that, in September 1998, I had the opportunity to see my dad for the first time since I had confronted him. I had no contact with him during those years. One of my sisters called to let us know that he had had a heart attack and his prognosis wasn't good. I felt very strongly that I needed to go see him. I had spent those six years walking through the healing process. I had done the work of forgiving him so that I could be free. I no longer held those hurts in my heart. I had truly experienced healing.

He couldn't hurt me again since he could no longer be in my life without taking responsibility for his actions, asking for forgiveness and proving that he had changed his ways. He had done none of that. So, building a relationship with him wasn't even a remote possibility. Boundaries are necessary and wise.

Remember that forgiveness and trust are two very different things. It is also true that you can care for someone who isn't trustworthy or even safe. Caring for them doesn't mean they are in your life again. However, you can allow your heart to care about them. That is part of healing as well. It is freeing. It allows you to see and recognize their brokenness, weaknesses, frailties, torment, and struggles – their humanity.

It was with that perspective that I boarded a plane to go see my dad.

Friends from church had paid for the airfare, a hotel to stay in, a car to drive and food money for the trip. They had great expectations for what this trip held. I was excited as well. You see, I was about to face my dad not from a place of hurt or revenge. I had no desire to bring harm. I didn't go expecting anything from him. I went in order to find freedom from the bondage of abuse. I chose to believe that as I spoke words of forgiveness that it would release me and free me for eternity. I went to "put a stake in the ground," marking the day of my freedom!

I now found myself standing face to face with my dad. I looked him right in the eyes and by God's grace was able to wholeheartedly say "I love you, Dad. I love you." I repeated those words several times. For me, those words expressed forgiveness. I knew if I said, "I forgive you, Dad," it would have meant nothing to him, since he hadn't admitted to anything. I chose, "I love you," knowing that those words are not possible to express to someone who has hurt you so very deeply without first having walked through healing and forgiveness. That must come first.

Without healing and forgiveness, it is even dangerous to speak those words. It will block your healing and bury your feelings. Those words, as I said above, didn't mean I was going to establish a relationship with him. That wasn't possible. It simply meant "I am done; I will not carry this burden any longer."

If I hadn't chosen to walk in forgiveness, I would not have been able to say those words to him. And though he didn't receive me and he rejected my words, God honored my choice. When I turned and left that day, I literally and physically felt the burden I had been carrying lift off me. Waves of peace like I have never known before flooded my heart and mind. This lasted for several hours. I knew now that it was finished. I knew I was free.

I returned to my hotel room and praised God. I danced and sang praises to my God! I rejoiced in my newfound freedom. I felt new. I felt fresh. I felt light. The war was over. My soul's fight was won. My soul was completely the Lord's. Satan had no more power over me. His design of destruction in my life had been silenced.

I am so thankful that my choice to forgive didn't depend on my dad's response. It was proven in the genuineness of my own heart. Forgiving my dad wasn't for him, although if he had received my forgiveness his life, too, would have been drastically different. He chose to stay in the house that had imprisoned him. He chose to live in unrepentance. His unrepentance made my words impossible for him to understand, let alone receive.

I hadn't gone to that house expecting him to receive my words or forgiveness. I went there to speak those words and offer my forgiveness in order to collect my own freedom. You see, I went with a lot of work already complete in me. I had rewired my thinking patterns, placed responsibility where it belongs, mourned what I didn't have as a child, grieved the loss of my own child, and released the false guilt that riddled me throughout my life. I had also done the work of understanding and embracing forgiveness.

Each of those things was vital and integral to the completion of my healing. There is something powerful and final about actually speaking out loud the words of forgiveness to the one who caused the pain. There is something eternal about those words. I believe with those words; a spiritual transaction takes place. It is a transaction of "sending away" the hurts, wounds and pain and receiving peace in their place.

If it isn't possible to say the words of forgiveness directly to the person who hurt you, then write a letter, even if you don't mail it. Speak the words out loud. Saying the words out loud is powerful. It is taking back territory. It is fighting for your soul!

Remember the box? Forgiveness is sending the offense away. That day as I stood before my dad, I was saying in essence, "Dad, you hurt me in a devastating way. You injured me. You caused a great amount of pain. I have carried it for all these years. But today, I am letting you know, I am letting God know, I am letting Satan know and I am letting myself know that I refuse to carry this offense any longer! I forgive you. I am sending the offense away. I want to be free!"

Do you know what happens in heaven at that moment? God sees you. He sees your determination to be healed. It touches His heart. He bundles those offenses up and hurls them far away from you. He sends them to the abyss and covers them with His blood. He frees you!

Hang on, though! Don't stop reading. God is not done. No! The most mind-boggling thing starts to take place. You could miss it if you don't wait for it. Are you still reading? He then begins His work in you to transform you. He takes those hurts and turns them into good. Keep your eyes on Him or you will miss this miracle of all miracles.

It stuns me how people watch the sunset. They stop what they are doing in their lives for a few minutes and watch the sun disappear from the sky. Then, the most baffling thing happens. They get up and walk away. To me, they miss the most beautiful part of the sunset. They miss seeing the sky burst into color after color. They miss the miracle.

Don't do all the work and miss the miracle! The miracle is about to happen. You are about to witness how God can take brokenness and turn it into dancing. You are about to witness the burden turn into rejoicing. You are about to witness anger turn in compassion, darkness to light, ashes to beauty, shame to confidence, guilt to freedom, hurt to love. Don't miss it! Don't cheat yourself out of the gift of forgiveness. It truly is the sunset to the healing process. He delights in this moment in each of our lives. He delights to take what we have discarded and prove His character. He delights in showering us with good things in response to following His ways. It happened in my life and it can happen in yours.

At the New Year's Eve church service of 1998, I made a commitment to write to my dad every two months for a year. The deadline for the first letter to be written was February of 1999. I so wish that I could tell you that I wrote that letter on

January 1st or even January 31st, but no, I waited and waited, putting it off. Finally, the last Tuesday, yes, on the morning of the last Tuesday of February, I mailed the letter.

That very afternoon, a pastor from my church called me to ask if I would be willing to give my testimony to a church of ten thousand during four services that weekend. What amazing timing! I felt it was God honoring my obedience. I gave my testimony that Sunday and I now had ten thousand people holding me accountable throughout the year to continue with those letters. And believe me, they held me accountable! They would stop me and want an update and ask me when I would be sending my next letter. I loved their involvement!

My dad never responded to my letters. It didn't matter though. I had learned that forgiveness is neither based on emotion, nor determined by the other person's response. Forgiveness is a choice and its genuineness is proven within your own heart.

II Corinthians 1: 3-4 says: *"Praise be to the God and Father of our Lord Jesus Christ, the Father of compassion and the God of all comfort, who comforts us in all our troubles, so that we can comfort those in any trouble with the comfort we ourselves receive from God"* (NIV). That verse mirrors my heart! I so delight in being there for those who are hurting and speak hope into their lives. It is a hope that resonates within me. It is the most fulfilling experience in my life. It fills me with joy as I see again and again the faithfulness and love of God towards each person who seeks healing in their lives. That is redemption. That is the sunset of healing!

~ A Shift ~

Several months after the trip to see my dad, I was in a church service. The message was on the portion of scripture where Peter was fishing after the resurrection of Jesus.

When they had finished eating, Jesus said to Simon Peter, "Simon son of John, do you love me more than these?" "Yes, Lord," he said, "you know that I love you."

> *Jesus said, "Feed my lambs."*
> *Again, Jesus said, "Simon son of John, do you love me?"*
> *He answered, "Yes, Lord, you know that I love you."*
> *Jesus said, "Take care of my sheep."*
> *The third time he said to him, "Simon son of John, do you love me?"*
> *Peter was hurt because Jesus asked him the third time, "Do you love me?" He said, "Lord, you know all things; you know that I love you."*
> *Jesus said, "Feed my sheep".* (John 21:15-17, NIV)

This exchange took place after Peter had denied Jesus three times as He walked the trail that led to His crucifixion. I had heard it and read it probably a thousand times. But Pastor Wayne explained in that service how Peter had lost his courage, not his love for Jesus. In that moment, tears flooded down my face. I realized with sadness and relief that on that day when my mom walked out of the abortion room, it wasn't due to a lack of love. It was because she couldn't face the reality that her daughter, who was impregnated by her own father, was about to have an abortion. In that moment, she had lost her courage. She didn't stop loving me at that moment. My mom loved God and was a devout Catholic. This moment wasn't supposed to happen. Not to her daughter, not by her husband. How could this have happened?

I now see my mom as a human being suffering a great tragedy. The only difference between her and me was that I couldn't physically walk out of that room. If I could have, I would have left running. But I now realized that she really did love me. That statement kept running through my mind and heart as I sat there wiping the tears from my face. I received her love that day. A shift occurred in my heart towards her.

I also came to understand at a later time that she was largely powerless to find help for us, since in the 1960s to 1980s, there was little or no societal recognition of domestic violence or sexual abuse. Police didn't take domestic disputes seriously. She was a mother of six children living in the suburbs. She was removed from her family of origin who lived in the city, had no driver's license, no access to public transportation, no job, and only a few friends. And all with a husband who worked from home; he was the ever-present eye on everything she did and spoke. Where could she possibly go? Who could she tell? Who would take in a mother with six children? She was trapped.

Even in today's society where there is more awareness and societal support systems, domestic violence is a difficult thing to be free from. The trap is the relationship itself. The partner knows how to demonstrate love as well as violence. It is those seemingly loving moments that cause deep confusion within the victim. They will often say, "But he loves me," "He said sorry," "He doesn't mean to hurt me," "It really is my fault, I need to watch what I say," and many more. The two people are connected to each other and do actually love each other. It isn't

---

See Appendix G for further information on domestic violence.

healthy love, however. It's a dangerous love. It's intoxicating.

If the one being abused reaches the point of wanting to leave, that is the most dangerous point in the relationship. All the abuser's insecurities which fuel the need for control in the relationship escalate, creating an even more volatile situation. Many victims have been either killed or seriously harmed when attempting to leave. Leaving must be carefully thought out and planned. There are two movies that capture this dynamic rather well: Sleeping with the Enemy and Enough. These movies show the dynamics that make it difficult to leave and the danger involved in doing so.

If you are in this situation, I would strongly encourage you to seek professional therapy where you will find help in making these choices carefully and thoughtfully. It is not something to be taken lightly or done on a whim. If you are a friend of someone going through this, please know that your friend can't "just leave." It's not possible. Getting him or her through the crisis will take great patience on your part. The best thing you can do is to support your friend and not push him or her into any choice along the way. Another way of showing your support is to educate yourself on this issue.

With this new perspective on my mom, I wrote this letter to her. I wrote it from my heart, as an expression of forgiveness. You can forgive from your heart at any time in your life. Many people hold the belief that in order to forgive someone, that person has to be alive. It isn't true. I experienced a release of the hurt on the day that I wrote this letter. Relationships live on in our hearts and minds long after a person's death. It is possible to resolve those relationships within your own heart. It isn't worth holding onto the hurts. It only hurts you.

Here is what I wrote:

Dear Mom,

Oh, Mom, how I love you! The other day I came across a picture of you and me. It was at my college graduation. My head was resting on your shoulder – resting in complete peace and joy. Your face was beaming with joy and pride!

You really were a great Mom! I know that being a Mom was everything to you. I understand that feeling now. That is what I want, too. Perhaps some of it is a spillover from all the special moments I've missed out on with Todd Jacob. So many times, I picture him, or I just want to touch him, hold him, and love him. But I know that you are taking good care of him now.

Mom, I miss you. Memories of what life was like are slowly coming back – good memories. The memories you created for us, like the baking, the garden, going to church, sitting around talking with each other. Mom, I am so sorry for all the ways I hurt you. I wish that somehow the abuse and the abortion didn't have to come between us for so many years. I know life changed for us after the abortion. Those were hard years. But even during that time, I know that you loved me. I wish we could have talked about it. But we all went on in silent pain. I developed epilepsy-you developed cancer and Dad? Well, he just went on.

Mom, you had so much courage. I see that now. I see how desperately you tried to give us a "normal" life amid the horror and chaos that Dad brought to our family.

Thank You, Mom, for everything that you did for us – for the things I know about and the things I don't know about. Mom, I know in your heart you wanted so much more than what we received. That must have broken your heart. You worked so hard to give us so much and

Dad would just come along and destroy it with his anger, violence and abuse.

With silent resolution, you would pick up the pieces of our lives and reassure us that all would be okay and try to rebuild the life you wanted for us. That, Mom, took bravery, courage, vision, and mostly great, great love! Thank You for all the times that your heart was filled with pain and yet you showed us nothing but love.

Your message did get through to us though. It wasn't for vain. All of us chose a good life, free from destruction and violence. Your bravery and courage were passed on to us by your spirit that still continues to watch over us.

As loud and destructive as Dad's anger was, your love and care were that much stronger. Your strength and love carried us through those horrific days. And I know that God was carrying you through too. God was watching over all of us because of your prayers for us.

I love you Mom and I truly wish you were still with us. I wish you could see our happiness. I wish you could see us on the other side of those horrible times. We all got through it. God has touched our lives and continues to heal us and make us whole. I wish you could share these times.

Each of your children are who we are today in honor and tribute to who you were to us during all those years. Your effect on us is lasting. Dad's effect has blown away. That would be remarkable if it were true of just one of us, but the fact that it is true of all of us is truly astounding! Well done, Mom!

Thank you, Mom, for your love, strength, courage and bravery. Thanks for believing in us.

I look forward to spending eternity with you.
Love,
Your daughter

I am now at peace with my mom. I truly do look forward to seeing her again in heaven. I am assured of seeing her there since she demonstrated her faith in Jesus. I have followed in her footsteps in my own life. My faith in God is a vital faith for me. My faith has steered me through life, sustained me through difficult times, inspired me, and given me purpose. I am forever grateful to my mom for instilling faith in me from a young age.

~ Forgiving Self ~

As I mentioned earlier, the hardest part of my journey of healing was forgiving myself for the abortion. I held onto a profound sense of guilt and shame. I felt unlovable. I didn't feel worthy of forgiveness from others, God, or myself. I felt I had committed the worst possible act imaginable. How does someone come back from that?

It took a long time to just untwist the fact that I didn't choose to have an abortion. It took a long time to be able to place the responsibility on my dad, where it belonged, for causing my pregnancy in the first place. It took a long time to place responsibility on my mom for resorting to this "solution." It took years for me to place the responsibility where it rightly belonged. It was a part of replacing unhealthy thoughts with healthy ones. Even with that work done, my emotions wreaked havoc on me. Instead of reminding myself that it wasn't my fault, I kept audience with my emotions such as the guilt, shame, insignificance, worthlessness, et cetera. I allowed the emotions to prevent me from forgiving myself. I punished myself through my emotions.

I have talked to many women who had an abortion. From those stories as well as my own, it is plain to see that it brings destruction to all involved. It has a sting. The sting has captured many women and men in its snare. Once in the snare of guilt and shame, it is difficult to win the battle.

Abortion's sting has been known to cause the following symptoms:

135

"...*guilt, depression, grief, anxiety, sadness, shame, helplessness and hopelessness, lowered self-esteem, distrust, hostility toward self and others, regret, sleep disorders, recurring dreams, nightmares, anniversary reactions, psycho-physiological symptoms, suicidal ideation and behavior, alcohol and/or chemical dependence, sexual dysfunction, insecurity, numbness, painful re-experiencing of the abortion, relationship disruption, communication impairment and/or restriction, isolation, fetal fantasies, self-condemnation, flashbacks, uncontrollable weeping, eating disorders, preoccupation, confused and/or distorted thinking, bitterness, and a sense of loss and emptiness.*" (Rue's publication as cited in Alcorn, 2000, p. 195)

I can count many of these symptoms as a part of my own experience. It is quite a list of possible negative responses. Abortion is a violent experience that not only physically tears a living fetus from its mother's womb, but also tears apart the mother's soul. It is a devastating price to pay. It lays a mine field that often proves impossible to navigate, leaving the mother and father destroyed in its wake. It has torn families apart, pitting daughter against parents, girlfriend against boyfriend, wife against husband, friend against friend. At times, the woman simply suffers in silence, alone, allowing her own soul to be eroded in the process. As her soul is eroded, her relationships suffer, since she can't possibly be the person she is meant to be for her loved ones.

Research shows that these negative effects aren't felt by a select few. Alarmingly, they affect a staggering number of women.

"Longer term studies have found that 10 to 30 percent of abortion patients experience serious ongoing psychiatric problems. In one five-year study: 25 percent of women who had undergone abortion surgery sought out psychiatric care, as opposed to 3 percent of women with no prior abortions. Another study found that psychiatric disorders were 40 percent more common among women who had abortions than among those who hadn't." (Ashton's publication as cited by Alcorn, 2000, p. 197)

I asked many women who have had abortions and the men who fathered these children how long they held onto their pain. It was astounding to hear that many of them held onto their pain for over twenty years. Interestingly enough, research shows that *"psychiatrist(s) frequently hear expressions of remorse and guilt concerning abortions that occurred twenty or more years earlier. In one study, the number of women who expressed 'serious self-reproach' increased fivefold over the period of time covered by the study."* (Reardon's publication as cited by Alcorn, 2000, p. 197)

It can clearly be said that time does not heal all wounds. In fact, the more time that goes by with one suffering in silence, the more detrimental it is to the soul. Holding on to a secret as powerful as an abortion can be enough to cause psychiatric damage.

In my journey of healing and in many women's lives that I have had the privilege of talking with, it was of paramount importance to acknowledge our lost children. For me, it was placing the name that haunted me, "Todd Jacob," and writing a letter to him. For others it is making a memorial object, holding a memorial service even several decades after the abortion, saying a prayer of dedication to God to care for their child, writing a song, performing a dance, or many others. The ideas are endless and should be rather personal.

In April 2024, now living in Lancaster, PA, I found a special Memorial Garden for infants lost in miscarriage, SIDS, or stillbirth. It has a very moving statue of a woman and Jesus sitting on a bench turned towards each other and holding hands. Jesus is holding the baby in His other hand and the woman is holding a heart necklace. The woman's face depicts peace, healing and a deep desire to hear from Jesus. The face of Jesus is filled with compassion and joy. When I saw this statue, it brought me to tears. I was once again reminded of His love and healing. The garden also has little name tags for babies that have been lost in the manners mentioned above. Since those weren't how Todd Jacob was lost, I didn't feel right about having a tag made for him. However, it did raise awareness within me that it was important for his name to exist somewhere in this world. I looked up options a few weeks later and found one that would work for me. I ordered a ceramic red tulip (remember my tulip story?) that came with a customizable tag for the person's name on one side and a message on the other side. It was a moving experience to choose this, order it, and for the first time ever, hold something physical that held his name on it. There are no words to describe what it was like to see the name of Todd Jacob while holding the tulip and tag in my hands. I'm beyond grateful that God's healing is timeless and ongoing. He is constantly pursuing every depth of healing that He bought on the cross!

It is **never** too late to engage in some type of activity to resolve the many emotions tied to an abortion. It is significant to name your child and to perhaps find a way to have your child's name exist in this world. The key is to acknowledge the existence of the child since the act of abortion at its core steals away the child's dignity and personhood. Returning that sense of dignity and acknowledging the child's existence often releases guilt and shame.

I would encourage you to also find a trustworthy friend to share your story with and to ask them to be involved in the memorial activity. Involving someone else will help with releasing the pain and heartache you hold. Be sure the person you involve is someone who will speak encouragement and forgiveness towards you. Condemnation and judgment do not facilitate healing. Choose wisely who walks with you.

Forgiving yourself is a task we all face. It is a part of our human experience. Maybe it isn't because of an abortion that you face the difficult journey of forgiving yourself. Perhaps it is a form of betrayal, a lack of courage, putting yourself first, lying, stealing, gossip, sinister words, or any others. Are you ready to place them at the feet of the only one who is able to forgive you to the depths of your being? Are you ready to go to Him to find the strength to change your ways? Are you ready to walk in healing towards others? He is! He waits for you as well! He waits with open arms, a compassionate heart, and healing words.

As you go to Him and are embraced by Him, remember to gaze upon His hands that bear the scars of the nails and look upon his feet that remind us of His sacrifice for us. Take in his brow that holds the story of His love. Receive His forgiveness. Receive the gift that He purchased for you. It cost Him everything, but He extends it to you freely. If you truly receive His forgiveness, it will be impossible to continue to condemn yourself.

I speak forgiveness over you. I speak bondages broken in the name of Jesus. I speak freedom over you. Walk in it! Be free. Know the One who has forgiven you. Know the name of Jesus!

I want to share the letter I wrote to Todd Jacob.

Dear Todd Jacob,

I love you so, so much! Though I have never seen you or even heard you cry, I know you!

I felt you in my womb. I thought about your tiny hands and feet. I have searched for you in every child's face, but I can't seem to find you.

Oh, Todd, can you ever forgive me? I didn't want to hurt you. I didn't want to kill you. I died inside the day that you died.

I have often hoped that somehow you were still in my womb, waiting to come into the world. But I know that you are in a much better place. You are with your Creator – our God!

Sometimes, I feel like a hypocrite. I say I am a Christian and that I love God and yet my own child didn't see one day of life.

I know the circumstances and that somehow allows me to reason the guilt away. But the fact remains, I could have prevented it. You were inside ME! I could have refused to get up on the table and just walked away.

Todd, forgive me. I love you! Please, don't hate me.

I often think about what you would be like now. I guess you would be about 10 or 11. What a big guy!

Todd, what do you look like? Do you have dark hair or light hair? Brown eyes or blue eyes? What do you like to do? What is it like up in heaven for you? Can you play baseball or soccer? Are there other boys like you in heaven?

I wish I had a picture of you. I wish I could hear your voice. I wish I could hear your feet go pitter -patter! I wish I could hold you close and tell you that I love you!

Do you have scars on your skin from what happened to you? I hope not.

Todd, when I think of what happened, the hurt is so bad that I have to shut it off. Please don't be offended by that.

You know, Christmas is very close and my class along with many others are putting on a Christmas program. I have thought a lot about you. I would have loved to have seen you be in a school play, singing with your sweet voice. I would have been so proud.

Todd, I would have loved you and taken care of you and raised you in the way of the Lord.

Todd, have you met my mom? She is in heaven now, too! If you do see her, tell her I love her too! I am so glad you are both in the best place possible. It must be incredible to be in His presence and to know Him completely.

I love you, Todd!
I look forward to the day when I can see you and hold you!
Will you let me hold you?
I promise I won't hurt you.

Love,
Mom

I remember the day I wrote this letter. It was about a year and a half after all my memories had returned. It was the end of the day and I was sitting in the quiet and empty first grade classroom that I taught in. My class had been preparing for the Christmas season including decorating the room, practicing our play, singing songs, and making gifts and cards for our loved ones. The children in my class that year were a Godsend to me. They each had an amazing capacity for loving one another and for loving me. It was a healing year for me, and often those healing moments came through the innocent words from my students.

This day, the memories of Todd Jacob were poignant and the sadness in my heart was deep. At this point I had of course assigned the name that floated in my mind to the child of my abortion. But I hadn't addressed him in any way. I felt the great need to express my heart to him and frantically looked around the room for some paper. I grabbed some old math worksheets and started writing on the back of the papers.

The words came so fast that my hand could barely keep up. Tears blinded me and tissues filled the floor and desk. I was a mess. Once I was done writing the letter, I sighed deeply. I read it over and over again out loud, allowing the words to sink in while at the same time releasing the hurt and pain for the first time in my life. It was a powerful experience. It was as if I had surgery to remove the toxins from my body. As this process ran its course for the evening, I wiped my tears, cleaned up my face, and picked up the numerous tissues that cluttered the desk and floor.

Naming him, writing a letter, and reading it out loud was an integral part of the healing process for me. It is one that can't be skipped over. Without giving dignity to Todd Jacob,

I don't believe the healing could have started. The first steps towards receiving God's forgiveness and forgiving myself had been taken.

Another important step in my healing process concerning the abortion came through two life-changing books: I'll hold you in heaven by Jack Hayford and Tilly by Frank Perretti. The first one is a short but powerful book that walks the reader through the biblical view by answering common questions regarding the loss of a child – whether that loss occurred through abortion, miscarriage, still birth or SIDS. It is written in a gentle manner with no condemnation or judgment. The second one is written as a novel and will hit home to anyone who has lost a child regardless of the cause. It is a healing and compassionate book. It is an easy read but one that will usher healing into your soul.

I read both books often to remind myself of His forgiveness when the emotions come to claim me. This part of the journey is, I believe, in some ways a forever one. It doesn't haunt me, it isn't a part of my daily, weekly or even monthly life, but from time to time it is there. The nightmares are long gone, the seizures have ceased, and the guilt is washed away. However, when the sadness comes back, I spend time with it. I don't run from it, I don't crumble, and I don't start all over again. I know I am forgiven, and I enjoy reminding myself of that when I need to. These books help me with that part. They are never far from my reach.

It is rare that I can share about this without being emotional. It is a sorrow; it is a loss. The grief of losing a loved one never really goes away. You simply adjust to that person not being around anymore. You go on loving them and missing them. That is what the sorrow in my heart is all about. I miss him.

I miss what I didn't have. I miss who he would have been. I miss the laughter and tears. I miss the accomplishments and the failures. I miss his essence. Sorrow isn't the same as condemnation. I don't feel judged. I feel sad. It is the sadness that connects me to him.

I want to remind you that there is forgiveness being extended to you by God through Jesus Christ. He doesn't hold this against you. He doesn't count you as unworthy. He doesn't turn from you. He has been pursuing you. He knows the depth of your hurt and pain and He is broken for your brokenness. His heart cries out to you. He desires that you know Him, bring the pain to Him, and dare to believe that He can heal it. I can tell you that He healed my pain and He can do the same for you. Once you grasp the depth of his complete forgiveness it will be easier to forgive yourself as well.

I look forward to the day that I will meet Todd Jacob in heaven, when I can walk with him and know him. I look forward to holding him, talking with him, laughing with him, and playing with him. I look forward to spending time with him. I look forward even more to spending time with him and my mom! Won't that be an amazing moment: all three of us together walking in love and forgiveness towards each other? Oh, I ache inside for that day. I hope that Dad can join us too. Now that would be a day to remember! I do hope and pray that my dad in his last breath prayed to receive Jesus Christ as his Lord and Savior. Could it be?

See Appendix C for resources on healing from an abortion.

~ Prayer ~

When I was a mere four or five years old, after a particularly violent night in our home, Mom came to our room to say goodnight. I leaned over the edge of the bed to give her a kiss and a hug. As I released her, I looked her in the eyes that were filled with pain and said "Mom, he just needs God in his life. I am going to pray for him until He chooses God." With as much of a smile as she could muster, she responded "You do that." From that moment on, I committed myself to pray for my dad. Pray, I did.

Thirty-one years later, having faithfully lifted him up in prayer, my dad died with no sign of having accepted Christ into his life. I was puzzled and struggled with this for years. I didn't understand why I felt heavily compelled all this time to pray for him if there would be no repentance. I fully know that he has his own free will and my prayers do not guarantee the desired response. Still, I wondered, what was it all for?

One day as I was praying about this once again, I heard God's still small voice say, *"The burden to pray for him was not for him. I placed that burden on you so that when the time came for you to forgive him, your heart would be ready."*

Buckets of tears streamed down my face as I realized how God had protected my heart so far back into the darkness. You can't pray for someone and not care for them. It's impossible. Praying for someone changes how you view them. I viewed my dad as someone who was in great need of God. I would need to forgive him one day to be free of all the hurt and bondage he created. I am certain that forgiveness wouldn't have come if I had not spent thirty-one years praying for that man. For-giveness only comes from a heart that is open.

Following his death in 2003, all but one of my siblings gathered at the house. It was in such bad shape that each of us had to wear two dust masks over our mouth and nose in order to breathe safely – and we still developed some breath-ing difficulties for a few days afterwards. He hadn't kept the house up in any way. There were places where a person could stand outside, place their hand through a hole in the wall and it would go all the way through to the inside of the home. It was evident that he had resorted to spending all his time in the smallest bedroom in the house with a space heater to warm the room. He had stacked dozens of piles of books around the room to pass the time. His bed sheets were torn in many spots. It was a sad reality of his last days.

One of my sisters drew my attention to something right by the head of the bed. It was my journal, open to a page where I had written about my choice to commit my life to Jesus Christ as my Savior! This was astounding for many reasons. When I moved to Hawaii after my mother's death, most of my pos-sessions remained at this house. At the time of his death, not one other item of mine could be found. I hadn't been back to the house from the day I left for Hawaii. I was stunned that he had kept anything of mine. It took my breath away that he not only kept this journal, but had it by his bed, open to that particular page! He had been reading it! I am amazed that of all the things my dad chose to keep of mine, he chose that journal.

I am assuming he threw my things away soon after I con-fronted him with the fact he had abused me. If I had been a fly on the wall, what would I have seen when he was throwing my things away? Was he throwing things out in a rage? Was he cursing me as he tossed one thing after another of mine in the garbage? Probably. And then what? He grabbed for the journal; it was in his hand. What caused him to say, "I think I will keep this"? Or did it somehow escape his notice until sometime later? How did that happen? I would love to know. How did God intervene in that moment? I am amazed that God chose to use a journal entry of mine from years past to possibly speak to his heart. Just the thought of it brings tears to my eyes. Of all things. How simple!

Could it be that in the end, he had prayed a prayer? Had he given his life to Jesus? Is he in heaven now? Oh, I do hope so. I had prayed for that without ceasing throughout my life. I prayed for his salvation even amid all the horrible memories and pain. I prayed for him even when I was angry with him. I prayed for him even in the pain of betrayal. I prayed for him, and in praying for him I was healed.

Several years after the first edition of this book, I had a spiritual dream. In the dream my entire family of origin were gathered together under a huge crisp white tent with white lights all around its perimeter. Under the tent was a huge banqueting table filled with an abundance of the best of foods. My dad, my Mom, my siblings, and I were all thoroughly enjoying each other's company. There was laughter, joy and peace in the air. My dad was dressed to the hilt in a very expensive suit and tie and shiny shoes. His countenance was breath taking as there was light, hope, joy, love and peace all over him. The dream zoomed in on him as he sat in a chair and faced me with compassion in his eyes and voice. He said to me, "Josee, I'm so deeply sorry for everything I did to you and all the devastation it brought you. I'm sorry for hurting you in so many ways. I was completely wrong to have abused you. I'm very sorry. Thank you for forgiving me. I know that was hard for you to do. I have received your forgiveness and God's forgiveness. I'm here in heaven because of that forgiveness. Thank you for that gift."

Wow! Wow! Wow! What an incredible dream! It's a dream I will never forget. It's a dream that fills me with deep hope that God did indeed answer my prayers of thirty-one years and that my dad, at some point in his life, gave his life to Christ. Praise the Lord! I rejoice in that!

A part of me, though, struggled to fully believe the dream was from God, after all, why wouldn't I want that dream. Was it from me or from God? Then, a few years after my dream, God, in His amazing grace, confirmed the dream was from Him. Someone who knew only the basics of my history shared that she had a dream the night before. The dream was the exact same dream down to the smallest of details! Her dream ended before my dad's words, since she didn't need to hear those words. Those words were for me. Her dream was what I needed to firmly receive it from God. It came from a very unexpected place. I felt it was God saying, "I meant that dream. I gave it to you. It is my gift to you. Your Dad is safely with me. All is well."

By faith, I firmly believe my dad gave his life to Christ and is therefore saved and redeemed in heaven. I do look forward to seeing him again there. I can't wait to stand before Jesus with my dad at my side rejoicing in His miraculous work in and through both of us. Praise the Lord!

There is truly not one thing that is outside the cross or bigger than the cross of Jesus Christ. All things and all people are in His hands and He can turn any heart towards Him. He can turn any circumstance to bring healing and growth within us.

Isaiah 61:3 says,

"Beauty for ashes.
The Oil of Joy for mourning.
The Garment of Praise for the spirit of heaviness.
That we might be called trees of righteousness,
   the planting of the Lord.
That He might be glorified."

That passage of Scripture captures the redeeming work of Jesus in my life. He can do this in your life as well!

See Appendix A for a prayer of salvation

The Soul's Fight

~ Waves of Trouble ~

The following is one of my journal entries.

Troubles are a part of life. They will always be a part of our lives. Sometimes they are loud and consuming and threaten to defeat us. Troubles are like waves that come crashing up against the rocks. They are constant, they can be expected. But when the wave goes washing back out, the rock is still there. The wave may have come with a loud voice. It may have forcefully come up against the rock or even completely covered the rock. BUT, when the wave went back out, the rock stood firm. It was in the exact spot it was before the wave even came.

When the troubles of life come with a loud voice eager to wash up against us or consume us, how can we be found to be like the rock that stood firm when the trouble washes back out?

Our foundation needs to be in Jesus Christ-the SURE foundation. Jesus is the solid rock. If our foundation is in Him, we have a guarantee that we will stand firm against troubles of all kinds! Our trust needs to be fully in Him so that we can grow strong and become, in Him, like a strong rock. If we have Jesus as our foundation, we will be able to stand our ground and look troubles right in the face without fear, but with the confidence that the battle has already been won!

How can we become strong in Him? By being with Him, hearing Him and studying His Word!

The one and only desire God has is to spend time with us. He created us for that very purpose. He sent His spirit for that very purpose. He just wants to spend time with us. He wants us to know Him, to love Him, and to seek Him. He wants to teach us all about Himself so that we can grow strong and be able to have joy in our hearts when troubles come. If we know who Jesus is, if we know His character, then when troubles come we will not be washed out. We will be able to stand firm with joy in our hearts because our trust in Him will not falter. When we call out to Him, He will hear and deliver us from all of our troubles.

Why can we 'count it all joy', when various trials come? Because we know that trials produce perseverance and when perseverance has its perfect result, we will be perfect, complete, lacking in nothing!' James 1:2-4

After many trials come our way we begin to see that, in Christ, we made it through. We begin to see that at every step Christ was there supplying our every need. As our eyes are opened to this, our trust in God is deepened and we become more solid, and our walk becomes straighter and stronger. Perseverance has begun within us. As this process continues our outlook on troubles changes from fear to confidence, from dependence on self to dependence on Christ, from something that must be endured to an opportunity to prove God's character! 'Perseverance has had its perfect result, causing us to become perfect, complete, and lacking nothing!!' James 1: 2-4

Loud consuming waves become instruments to chip away unneeded human tendencies and leave behind only a Godly vessel ready to be poured out into other people's lives.

What once was something feared turns into something that glorifies God! It brings glory to Him because we are now able to fight for our soul and be a mighty warrior for Him!"

It surprses me now to read this journal entry. The timing in which I wrote it astounds me even more. I wrote this following my three grand mal seizures in November 1991 and before I stood on the school grounds looking out onto the ocean in April 1992, realizing I had to face my past. On the day I wrote this journal entry, I remember sitting on the ocean wall watching the waves. I became focused on the rocks that would disappear and then reappear at the ebb and flow of the waves. I felt like those rocks, consumed, overwhelmed, drowning and not sure if I would be okay.

I felt the threat of the memories like the force of the waves crashing over the rocks. I was scared and uncertain of what the memories would do to me. I was afraid of being consumed by them. Somehow, as I sat on that wall watching those waves, God comforted me and I gained a glimpse of the path I would walk to my freedom. Hidden in this journal entry is knowing the character of God, being created for a purpose, God wanting to know us, a picture of being a vessel to impact other's lives and having to fight for our soul. Do those themes sound familiar? It was almost like a treasure map to the gems that I would find along my path of healing.

Your path will be filled with gems beyond your imagination. They will be deeply personal. They will be tailor-made for you by the Living God who created you, who knows every detail of your hurts, who weeps for you and with you, and who holds the keys to your healing. In the end you will be glad you traveled this path. You will never be the same again. There will be a joy upon you as you become free of the hurts and pain and to embark in who you are meant to be.

Whatever your journey will entail, I know the main ingredient will be forgiveness. It is my deepest prayer that through reading this book and taking a new look at forgiveness, you now have a better understanding of the true nature of forgiveness and will embrace the gift that lies within it. Forgiveness is, I believe, largely misunderstood. But when the beauty of the gift of forgiveness becomes apparent, it is compelling. I have found nothing else that offers freedom to the soul like forgiveness does. It is complete in its work and it transforms you into who you were meant to be.

I encourage you with a prevailing sense of urgency to both receive the gift of forgiveness and to extend the gift of forgiveness. It is a profound gift with many facets. It is full of priceless gems. I will never be glad that I had to go through my childhood hurts and wounds. However, I can honestly and firmly state that I would never trade the hurt for anything. The treasures I have gained from my healing, rooted in forgiveness, is beyond anything I could ever have dreamed of. It was worth every moment of pain. It was worth the struggle. It was worth the fight, the soul's fight. It brought me to the most amazing relationship with the Living God. And that is worth everything to me!

God is calling. He is calling to you in a way that is meaningful to you. Every illustration that I shared in this book was a real experience for me that was rich with meaning. God knew what I would respond to, what pictures would speak to me. He knows you, too. He is speaking to you. He is waiting for you. Are you ready? Do you desire to experience God in ways that you have never imagined before?

Seek Him and He will make Himself known to you. His voice is compelling. Your soul will be satisfied. Find Him and you will be saved and healed. Your purpose will be revealed. There will be harmony in the music and a rhythm to the dance. There is hope. I hold that hope for you with eager and great anticipation of your healing. It is the best path worth walking with the only One that can heal you: Jesus Christ.

The Soul's Fight

Appendices

The Soul's Fight

Prayer for Salvation

Beginning or renewing a relationship with Jesus Christ is all about acknowledging our humanity and the limits of our humanity. We have all caused hurt or harm to others at some point in our lives. We may have even caused harm to ourselves. All those moments were caused by choices that we made. Those choices are considered sin in God's eyes. Sin has a way of causing distance in our relationships, including our relationship with God. But Jesus Christ died on the cross to pay for our sin and, in so doing, eliminated the distance between Him and us. He desires a relationship with each and every one of us. He created us and gave His life for us just so He can know us. That is a great and awesome love! It is a desperate love.

If you desire to begin a relationship with Jesus Christ or renew your relationship with Him, simply use your own words to let Him know your heart. Praying is simply talking to God. It is done in the same way that we talk with one another. He delights in prayers that are honest, genuine and authentic. It isn't about impressive words, lots of words or even memorized words. It is about putting into words what is going on in your heart and soul. There are no wrong words. He knows before you speak what you will say. Praying is as much for the one praying as it is for God. There is something that happens when we speak our heart to the Heavenly Father. It is powerful. It is eternal.

Once you have prayed to begin a relationship with Jesus Christ or to renew that relationship, it is also important to tell someone you trust and who can guide you in your next steps, such as becoming active in a local church. It is vital that someone in your life knows your decision and can support you at this significant time in your life. You will need encouragement as well as someone to keep this decision important to you as you navigate through life. You will have many questions regarding how this decision, this new relationship, will impact your life. Your friend will be an important part of that journey.

If you are not sure what to pray, let me guide you. Please remember, though, you do not have to use these exact words. You can read through the following prayer to understand the basic concept, then form your own words in prayer. Whichever method you choose, be authentic.

"Jesus Christ, I acknowledge that I have sinned throughout my life and that You are the only one who can forgive me of my sins. I acknowledge that You died on the cross for my sins, thereby granting me the gift of forgiveness. I choose to receive that gift of forgiveness. I desire to begin a new relationship with You as my Savior and Healer. I pray that You will be with me throughout my life. Amen. "

If you just prayed that prayer or used your own words to begin a relationship with Jesus Christ, I would like to welcome you to the Kingdom of God! Jesus is dancing for joy that you want a relationship with Him. There is great joy taking place in heaven because of your decision. Now, tell a friend!

Sexual Abuse

What is sexual abuse?

Sexual abuse is any unwanted sexual contact, whether that activity is visual, verbal or physical. Consent is the key issue that determines whether sexual activity is abusive or not. Consent has many factors that must be considered. Those factors include the following.

- Consent must take place free of intimidation, force, bribery, or fear of consequences.

- All parties must be of legal age to consent. State laws differ from state to state regarding the age of consent.

- There must be a level of understanding (intellectually and emotionally) of what is taking place.

- Dependency is a factor, whether due to age (children or elderly) or a disability

- Power and status impact the ability to consent. For example, a boss who initiates sexual activity with a subordinate creates an unequal dynamic and takes away the freedom of his/her employee to refuse the sexual advances.

- Physical strength of all involved

How prevalent is it?

- On average, there are 463,634 victims (age 12 or older) of rape and sexual assault each year in the United States.

- 1 out of every 6 American women has been the victim of an attempted or completed rape in her lifetime (14.8% completed rape; 2.8% attempted rape).

- About 3% of American men—or 1 in 33—have experienced an attempted or completed rape in their lifetime.

- 17.7 million American women have been victims of attempted or completed rape.

- 9 of every 10 rape victims were female in 2003.

Taken directly from the RAINN (Rape, Abuse and Incest National Network) website:

Types of sexual abuse

Exposing a minor or non-consenting party to visual sexual abuse such as:

- Pornography

- Sending nude pictures of yourself or others via any electronic tool or a hard copy

- Exposing of genitals

- Forcing a person to watch sexual activity of any kind.

- Observing another person's nude body without their consent

- Videotaping any sexual activity without consent

Exposing a minor or non-consenting party to verbal sexual abuse such as:

- Sexual remarks of a person's body

- Sexually charged words via teasing, jokes, name calling, graphic sexual descriptions

Exposing a minor or non-consenting party to physical sexual abuse such as:

- Touching or fondling
- Excessive physical restraint or tickling that severely limits the movements of the other person
- Intercourse, oral sex, sodomy

Common symptoms of sexual abuse

- Insomnia/Nightmares
- Being zoned out
- Lack of healthy boundaries
- Memory block
- Anger
- Withdrawal
- Fear
- Depression
- Self-destructive behavior
- Risk-taking behavior
- Unexplained physical ailments
- Promiscuity or sexual difficulties
- Controlling or being controlled
- Pleasing others; performing
- Mistrust

According to the RAINN website, those who have been sexually abused are:

- 3 times more likely to suffer from depression
- 94% suffer from post-traumatic stress disorder
- 13 times more likely to abuse alcohol
- 10 times more likely to use major drugs
- 33% contemplate suicide
- 13% attempt suicide
- 70% experience moderate to severe distress, a larger percentage than for any other violent crime

Resources

If you are a victim of sexual abuse, I strongly encourage you to seek professional therapy in your local area. It is nearly impossible to get through your abuse by yourself. There are many resources available to you. Here a just a few.

- RAINN, the Rape, Abuse and Incest National Network (1-800-656-HOPE)
  www.http://www.rainn.org/

- Psychology Today has a directory of therapists across the country: http://therapists.psychologytoday.com/rms/

- American Association of Christian Counselors offers a directory of Christian Counselors across the country. https://aacc.net/

Abortion

Impact of an abortion

Abortions not only kill a living, breathing, developing human being, but also can cause destruction to both the mother and father of that fetus. The destruction left in the path of an abortion is devastating to say the least. The pain involved in this choice includes regret, guilt, shame, loneliness, suicidal thoughts, relational difficulties, isolation, grief, fear, a haunting emptiness, depression, anxiety and self-destructive behavior, to name a few.

The silence surrounding an abortion makes the pain and hurt even worse, since it imprisons the women alone forever. The emotions are denied just as the fetus was. The pain continues to grow, however. The silence is so powerful that it can potentially destroy the relationships of those who make this choice.

I know this pain intimately. I wish I didn't, but I do. I also know what it is to experience healing from the hurt. I know what it is to find the light in the darkness. I know what it is to be forgiven. I hold that hope for you as well. Healing is for everyone, not just those who somehow deserve it. I encourage you to be brave and silence the negative thoughts that keep you imprisoned. Courageously find your voice – a voice that gives dignity to your pain and dignity to the child you lost. Be brave and care for yourself by looking into the resources below. Be brave and contact them. Be brave and fight for your soul!

Resources

- Project Rachel
  http://www.hopeafterabortion.com/
  This Christian ministry also extends hope to those hurting in the aftermath of an abortion. They offer therapy, support groups, retreats and resources.

- Deeper Still
  https://deeperstill.org/
  This Christian ministry is across the country and ministers to women and men alike who are hurting from the aftermath of abortion.

- For crisis pregnancy or post-abortion counseling call 1-800-848-5683

Addictions

Addiction

The difference between someone who abuses substances or alcohol and someone who is addicted to them is determined by the physical reliance on the substance or alcohol. Abuse of drugs or alcohol certainly leads to addiction, due largely to the physiological response of the brain to prolonged use of substances, including alcohol.

Alcohol statistics

- Over 14.5 million people in the United States have an alcohol addiction.
- About 10.5% of children in the US live with an alcoholic mother or father.
- Alcohol related illnesses include a range of afflictions from developing cancers of the throat, larynx, liver, colon, kidneys, rectum, and esophagus, to immune system irregularities, brain damage, harming an unborn baby, and cirrhosis of the liver.
- 40% of alcoholism is inherited from an alcoholic parent.

All statistics were taken from the National Institute on Alcohol Abuse and Alcoholism website: niaaa.nih.gov

Substance abuse statistics

Among Americans aged twelve years and older, 37.309 million were current illegal drug users (used within the last 30 days) as of 2020.

- 13.5% of Americans 12 and over used drugs in the last month, a 3.8% increase year-over-year (YoY).
- 59.277 million or 21.4% of people 12 and over have used illegal drugs or misused prescription drugs within the last year.
- 138.543 million or 50.0% of people aged 12 and over have illicitly used drugs in their lifetime.
- 700K Drug overdose deaths in the US since 2000 are nearing one (1) million.

Statistics taken from https://drugabusestatistics.org

Resources

- SAMHSA: Substance Abuse and Mental Health Services Administration https://www.samhsa.gov/find-help/national-helpline
- Recovery Centers of America (Christian faith-based) https://recoverycentersofamerica.com/treatment/
- The Center: a place of hope https://www.aplaceofhope.com
- American Association of Christian Counselors Aacc.net
- Psychology Today has a directory of therapists across the country: http://therapists.psychologytoday.com/rms/

Suicide

Prevalence
Worldwide:

- An estimated 703,000 deaths by suicide a year worldwide.
- Over one in 100 deaths in 2019 were a result of suicide.
- The global rate of suicide is over twice as high for men than women.
- Over half (58%) of all deaths by suicide occur before the age of 50.

All these statistics are taken from the International Association for Suicide Prevention.

United States:

- 49, 476 people died of suicide in 2022.
- Suicide is the 4th leading cause of death among adults between 35-44 yrs of age.
- Suicide is the 3rd leading cause of death among 15 to 24-year-olds.
- Suicide is the 2nd leading cause of death among 25 to 34-year-olds.
- Suicide is the 11th leading cause of death in the United States.
- Ninety percent of those who take their lives have a treatable psychiatric disorder.
- There is a 4:1 ratio of males who successfully take their lives compared to females.
- There are 3x as many females then males who attempt suicide.

- In 2022, there were an estimated 1.6 Million suicide attempts.

All these statistics are taken from the American Foundation for Suicide Prevention (afsp.org)

Warning signs of suicide

- Loss of interest in activities
- Loss of appetite
- Depressed mood
- Low energy
- Either not sleeping or sleeping too much, hopelessness
- Withdrawal
- Talk of death, dying, not wanting to be alive anymore
- Putting affairs in order
- Giving away prized possessions
- Increased substance abuse
- No longer keeping up responsibilities at school or work
- Impulsive behavior
- Making a plan
- Access to means of taking life (pills, weapon, et cetera)

What to do

If you are experiencing thoughts of wanting to end your life:

- Please call or text the American Foundation for Suicide Prevention at 988. This is a 24-hour phone line with trained professionals ready to listen to you and give you support and resources.
- Call 911.
- Go to the nearest emergency room or psychiatric clinic.
- Tell a trusted friend or family member and allow them to find professional support for you.
- Tell your therapist about this and follow the therapist's guidance.

- Create a plan of who to talk to and what you can do when these thoughts overwhelm you, such as an art project, uplifting music, take a walk, build furniture, et cetera.
- Do not isolate yourself from others. You need support.

If you are a friend or family member of someone experiencing suicidal thoughts:

- Stay with them until professional support is involved.
- Take them to an emergency room or psychiatric clinic.
- Call 988, the American Foundation for Suicide Prevention.
- Listen, listen, listen.
- Take what they are saying seriously.
- Assure them that they aren't alone.
- Communicate that you understand that they feel hopeless, and that life is not worth living, but that you hold hope for them that life will get better.
- Remove items that could harm them.
- Follow up with them after their first visit with a psychiatrist/ therapist to ensure they continue to attend the sessions and are taking their medications.

Resources

- American Foundation for Suicide Prevention, call or text 988. (afsp.org)
- The Center: a place of hope. (aplaceofhope.com)
- Honey Lake Clinic. (honeylake.clinic)
- Psychology Today has a directory of therapists across the country. (Psychologytoday.com)
- American Association for Christian Counselors also has a directory of therapists across the country.

The Will and Testament of Our Lord Jesus Christ

Through the blood of Jesus Christ "we have obtained an inheritance, having been predestined according to His purpose who works all things after the counsel of His WILL" Ephesians 1:11

This is the inheritance of the Beloved:

1. _____ was chosen in Him before the foundation of the world. Ephesians 1:4
2. _____ is holy and blameless before Him. Ephesians 1:4
3. _____ was predestined for adoption. Ephesians 1:5
4. _____ has redemption through His blood. Ephesians 1:7
5. _____ has forgiveness for_____'s trespasses. Ephesians 1:7
6. _____ is alive together with Christ. Ephesians 2:5
7. _____ was raised up with Him. Ephesians 2:6
8. _____ is seated with Him in the heavenly places. Ephesians 2:6, Philippians 3:20
9. _____ is His workmanship, created in Christ Jesus for good works, which God prepared beforehand, that _____ should walk in them. Ephesians 2:10
10. _____ who was formally far off, has been brought near by the blood of Christ. Ephesians. 2:13
11._____ is a fellow citizen with the saints. Ephesians 2:19
12. _____ is of God's household. Ephesians 2:19
13. _____ has, through Him, access in one Spirit to the Father. Ephesians 2:18

ABOUT THE AUTHOR

The most important aspect of life to me is my faith in Jesus Christ. Faith in Jesus has been my foundation throughout my life no matter what came my way. Jesus has sustained, redeemed, and restored me. (Ruth 4:15) I would not be alive without Him in my life.

I am a Licensed Marriage and Family Therapist in Lancaster, PA. I earned my Master's Degree in Marriage and Family Therapy from Bethel Seminary, San Diego in 2003. The graduate program focused on integrating psychology and the Christian faith.

CONTACT INFORMATION:

Josee D'Amore is available for speaking engagements, professional therapy and consulting. Her professional therapy practice, Gems of Hope Counseling, is located at Petra Church in New Holland, PA.

Her area of focus includes trauma recovery, abuse recovery, anxiety, grief, physical illness, and co-dependency. She considers her role as a therapist to be a calling and a mission. She finds deep fulfillment in helping others find God-given peace, freedom, comfort, insight, confidence, and effective life skills in navigating life's challenges.

She can be contacted at joseedamore4@gmail.com.

Made in the USA
Middletown, DE
26 October 2024

63348725R00102